the encyclopedia of
cockatiels

george a. smith

Front cover: Photo by Harry V. Lacey
Back cover: Photo by Sam Fehrenz.

Frontispiece by Harry V. Lacey.

ISBN 0-87666-958-5

Contents

The cockatiel, *Nymphicus hollandicus* (Kerr)

Kingdom: Animalia
Phylum: Chordata
Class: Aves
Order: Psittaciformes
Family: Cacatuidae
Genus: *Nymphicus*
Species: *hollandicus*

Photos attributed to Manolo Guevara and Miceli Studios were taken through the cooperation of Paterson Bird Store (Totowa, New Jersey) and Novak's Aviaries (Deer Park, New York).

Introduction and Acknowledgments

There are several books wholly or partially concerned with the cockatiel. When asked to write yet another, it seemed that the only possible reply could be a refusal. However, on reading through the literature and remembering the queries raised by breeders and pet owners, it seemed that a good case could be made for a truly complete book that might provide some of the information that the others, somehow, never included. Indeed, my own early experience was recalled when I could not even find such basic information as to the length of the incubation period, how long cockatiels took to be mature, and whether the first molt shed all body feathers including, as I now know that it does, flight and tail feathers.

Most of the information in this book comes from personal experience. Whenever possible, statements have been checked with other breeders who have, in many cases, and especially with the color forms, provided me with fresh knowledge.

In the past the cockatiel has certainly been underrated both as a pet and as a subject for exhibition in cage-bird shows. The cockatiel makes an extremely docile pet. The male bird usually learns to mimic at least some words and phrases, is easy to care for, and is extremely hardy and long-lived. Up to the time of writing the National Exhibition of Cage Birds, which is usually billed as the largest cage-bird show in Britain, still has no classes for any color variety of cockatiel. It provides classes for zebra and Bengalese finches, birds which are, very likely, not as well-known to the general public and may well not be as numerous as are cockatiels.

Perhaps physical size may have something to do with this neglect. Cockatiels would require more exhibition space because of their larger cages. The breeders of zebra finches, Bengalese, canaries, and budgerigars usually make do with a not too large garden shed and an aviary or a few flight cages. The present-day cockatiel breeder, using the same equipment, could house only a few pairs. But cockatiels do well in cages and certainly breed in accommodations that, in proportion to their size, are no larger than those given to budgerigars.

Paradoxically, as cockatiels have never been previously selected for exhibition, they may prove to be ideal for this purpose. Today if they were exhibited, everyone would have an almost equal chance of breeding a winner. This is something that could never be said for exhibition budgerigars and canaries. With their long history of showing, the chance of a beginner's producing a good exhibition bird is not very high. More, if show points are drawn up the mistake of putting emphasis on size could be avoided with the hindsight of what has happened to the show budgerigar. Perhaps, as with "new-colored" canaries, most emphasis should be given to quality and color of plumage. This way the stamina and fertility of the wild cockatiel may be maintained.

In the course of writing this book I have become deeply indebted to many people for their help: Mr. J. Rice and Mrs. J. Newan loaned several of their cockatiels for photographing. Such a kindness in the middle of a breeding season cannot go unmentioned. Messrs. David Marriott, Bob Wilkinson, Bill Howarth, and Dr. and Mme. Swaenepoel, like Mr. Rice, are all very successful breeders of cockatiels, and each provided some of the genetic material. Lastly, Miss Rosemary Low of the weekly magazine *Cage & Aviary Birds* persuaded me that there was a need for such a book as this. To these people I would like to tender my utmost thanks. Any mistakes or misconceptions are my own and in no way stem from these good people.

8

What is a Cockatiel?

The cockatiel is a medium-sized Australian parrot with an erectile crest on the top of its head. It has so very readily taken to captivity that it is now extremely well-known as both a cage and aviary bird. Although it has been captive-bred for more than a century, it is only in very recent times that the cockatiel has come to exist in various distinctive color varieties giving them quite a different appearance from the wild-type grey. By the usual definition, such changes of color and the multiple generations of captive breeding can be said to have made the cockatiel into a fully domesticated bird.

Parrots are quite easily separated from other birds on account of their hooked beak, short neck and the curious feet that have two toes pointing forward and two backward. In avicultural literature one can often read of "parrot-like birds" or the just as clumsy-sounding and equally contrived "psittacines." By these circumlocutions the authors always seem to mean no more than "parrots" and use these jarring terms, just as the Americans sometimes use "hookbills," because they forget that "*parrot*," in the plural, is a general name for all members of the order, whether they be macaws, Amazon parrots, lovebirds, lories or parakeets.

Indeed, there simply are no parrot-like birds, although certain species may resemble parrots by some behavior pattern or feature of anatomy, such as the crossbills of northern forests and the turacos and colies of Africa. But if parrots do have any relationship with other living birds, it is accepted by the majority of ornithologists that this would be with the pigeons. This opinion is far from absolute for it hangs upon a frail evidence that is strengthened more by tradition

Although recent serological studies have led some taxonomists to conclude that parrots are more closely related to owls than to any other bird group, most taxonomists currently believe that pigeons are parrots' most closely related living relatives. Photo of owl at left by Mueller-Schmida; photo of pigeon by Dr. Herbert R. Axelrod.

The cockatiel is the smallest member of the cockatoo family (family Cacatuidae) and shares with its larger relatives the characteristic of having a movable crest. Each of the three Leadbeater's cockatoos shown here has its crest in a different attitude of erection.

than direct fact. Indeed there is perhaps almost equal evidence, including some very recent work on egg and blood proteins, that the owls may have a nearer kinship.

On account of their anatomy, cockatoos form one of the most readily accepted subdivisions of the parrots. The layman, who knows nothing of skeletons, skulls, powder-down patches and gall bladders, recognizes their distinction because of their movable crest and because they are black, white, yellow or pink and never have any blue, green or purple feathers, as do most other parrots. The cockatiel is the smallest of the cockatoos.

There is a considerable difference in the external appearance of the long-tailed cockatiel compared with the larger, more stockily-built, short-tailed cockatoos. Cockatoos typically have massive bills and can feed on seeds and fruits that because of their hardness are largely unavailable to other birds. Some cockatoos even use their strong bills to dig into the ground for tubers, bulbs and other buried vegetable foods. Some crack open branches to feed on wood-boring grubs. The cockatiel, however, is very different. It lives a nomadic existence searching for seeds and water in the arid central regions of Australia where it must be able cover vast areas by flying fast and for long periods. The budgerigar shares the same habitat as the cockatiel and eats much the same seeds, and both, having the same needs, have very much the same body shape.

After the budgerigar, which in the U.S.A. is more usually called the parakeet, the cockatiel is by far the most well-known species of parrot. Yet it has never achieved quite the popularity of the former. As a pet, the cockatiel does have certain advantages over the budgerigar. With its larger size it has a totally different personality in the same way, almost, that large dogs differ from the miniature breeds. It is more phlegmatic and an altogether stronger bird. The greater size may be partially responsible for the cockatiel's having a greater life-span. The caged budgerigar is said to have an average cage life of but four years, and a ten-year-old budgie is exceptional. Many cockatiels live to be twenty, and aviary-housed cockatiels of twenty-five are seen.

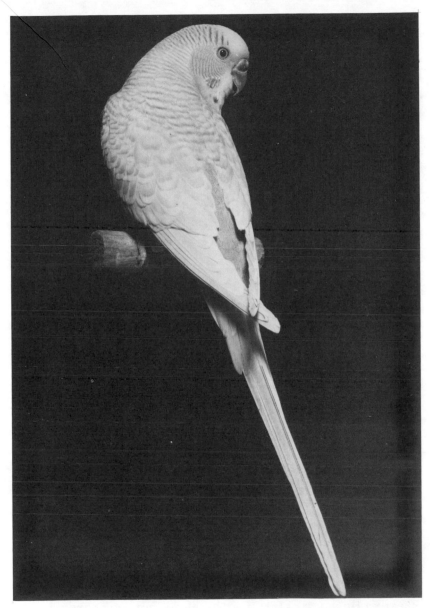

Much more commonly seen as a pet than the cockatiel is the budgerigar, or parakeet (*Melopsittacus undulatus*). One reason that the budgerigar is more often kept than the cockatiel is that it is a less expensive bird, but in general cockatiels are hardier and offer a greater degree of satisfaction to their owners. Photo by Harry V. Lacey.

A good example of the type of budgerigar bred for size and plumpness. Notice that the bird is actually sitting, rather than standing, on its perch. Photo by Harry V. Lacey.

Perhaps the short life of so many pet parakeets is because so large a proportion of them have some relationship to show birds. It is unfortunate that when show budgerigars are being judged considerable emphasis is put upon large size. In part this bulk has to come from excessive fat, not only because it is easier to select for obesity than for simply birds, but the show points are so framed as to actually prefer a corpulent budgerigar to a large, well-made, normally-proportioned one. The show budgerigar has now become the avian equivalent of an arctic seal or whale, for it is swathed in a great thickness of fat. It is, therefore, not a bit surprising that two of the commonest fatal disorders of pet parakeets are fatty tumors and obesity. This might well also explain their low fertility, for their configuration is a product of an endocrine imbalance; thyroid malfunction is also quite common.

14

Until now cockatiels have never been specifically bred for exhibition. The selection that has taken place seems to have been largely for increased fertility, even if most of this selection has been done quite unwittingly. The production of the color forms of the cockatiel has had the consistent aim of trying to produce as many as possible in the shortest amount of time. It appears never to have been exceptional to hear of some pairs rearing more than a dozen youngsters a year.

It is perfectly true that when they are taught to speak cockatiels may not be able to repeat the number of words, nor the multiplicity of noises, as can their gifted fellow-Australian, the budgerigar. Yet the sounds they do learn are mostly reproduced with a greater fidelity to the original. A point that adds greatly to the attraction of pet cockatiels is that they positively enjoy being stroked or tickled about the head. Nor will they mind much if they are stroked elsewhere or even picked up. This is quite different from the budgerigar, which will usually move off or fly away if an attempt is made to fondle them, and the bolder, more forceful ones may bite the approaching finger.

This considerable difference in familiarity of behavior comes because the parakeet, as with so many of the Australian parrots, has a natural unease about being touched by another bird. The only occasions when budgerigars voluntarily make contact are when they fight, during their courtship, when the cock bird feeds his hen, and, rather obviously, when they mate. Yet cockatiels, even though they may have almost as strong an instinct as the budgerigar for not touching another bird with their body, do actively preen each other's head. The desire to preen or be preened is very strong. Anyone who has a pet cockatiel soon learns to recognize when it pleads to have its head tickled or scratched by its drooping the head with the eyes partly closed.

Cockatiels can be taught not to particularly mind being picked up in the hand. Anyone who does this should first remember that a cockatiel bite can be a very painful business as they sometimes hold on and chew with a rat-like tenacity. The secret in picking them up is never to alarm the bird. All movements, as indeed with any other bird, should be done in

Unlike species that congregate in large numbers at one roosting spot, with the birds huddled against one another, cockatiels have a natural distaste for being forced into contact with their cagemates. Except when breeding or preening, they will always try to leave space between themselves. Birds forced into too-close contact because of the small size of their cage will be subjected to stresses that will affect their health and behavior. Photo by Manolo Guevara.

Well trained cockatiels enjoy human companionship. Instead of just allowing themselves to be picked up, they actually solicit attention from their owners and practically beg for such favors as having their heads scratched. Photo by Dr. Herbert R. Axelrod.

17

a quiet, slow, and precise way that minimizes alarm. They will be least frightened, because the constraint is minimal, when a hand is cupped over the body as they sit upon the other hand. Non-tame cockatiels, and birds loose in an aviary, can only be caught satisfactorily in a net. The net can also be used to transport them for short distances.

DESCRIPTION

The cockatiel, although considerably larger than the budgerigar, is still rather small, being about the same size as the starling. However, its much longer tail gives a length of about a foot from the beak to the tail-tip. As the several illustrations show, the wild-form is a dark grey color with a white band of feathers on the wing and a pretty patch of bright marigold-orange on the cheek. The head is capped by a crest, and the bill, eyes and feet are black. The coloring of the adult sexes is quite different, for the hens are much drabber and have a grey "wash" which covers the yellow and marigold colors of the head. Youngsters of both sexes are exactly similar to adult hens.

When he becomes adult, the male loses the black color on the sides and front of his head. This loss clears the yellow and orange that was masked when he was immature. Strangely, although the adult male has less black on the head, he now has far more black on the body; this intensifies the grey to a near blackness. Adult males also completely lose the ability to produce yellow bars on the wings and the yellow reticulation or netted effect on the tail. This loss of yellow on the wings and tail is of supreme value when it comes to sexing the pied and lutino mutations where the sexes of these are otherwise alike.

THE HISTORY OF THE COCKATIEL'S DOMESTICATION

Although it was first described in 1792, it took a very long while before the cockatiel was displayed as a live bird in Europe or America. This was largely because until the early years of the nineteenth century, Australia had only been settled in the small areas around the penal colonies. The

18

Male (left) and female cockatiel, showing the solid coloration of the underside of the male's tail feathers and the light areas on the female's tail feathers. Photo by Louise van Der Meid.

Regardless of their sex, young cockatiels resemble adult females. Shown above is a one-month cockatiel; below is an adult female. Photos by Dr. Gerald R. Allen.

A habitat of wild cockatiels at Beverley Springs, Western Australia.
Photo by Dr. Gerald R. Allen.

neglect of this continent was partly because it was half-way
around the world from Europe and could not therefore com-
pete with the greater attractions of the longer-settled, and
far nearer, North America which was also in need of colonists, and partly because Australia then appeared to have no
indigenous crops or mineral deposits worth exploiting.
True, the success of the introduced Merino sheep began to
bring pasturalists and capital into the recently discovered
extensive grazing lands several hundred miles from the settled coastal strip. But it was the discovery of gold, more than
anything else, that at last began to bring Australia the needed immigrants. Now that agriculture and avarice were working together, people began to arrive to exploit this empty
land and to develop it. The sailing ships that carried the wool
back could now return at least part-full, with a paying cargo
of passengers and of European-made goods.

Among the willing new colonists were the brothers-in-law of the English ornithologist John Gould. Gould was just then starting his very successful career as a compiler of really excellent natural history books. Most were books on birds where each species was carefully and most beautifully illustrated by lithographic hand-colored prints, rather like those of Audubon for North American mammals and birds but in more realistic poses and with far better background studies.

The stuffed skins that his Coxen relatives and other collectors had so recently sent back to British museums whetted Gould's appetite for more. A very great proportion of these species of birds were completely unknown to science, and this would put whoever could first describe them in an especially advantageous position, as eminence in the world of ornithology then could be largely earned by the number of new species a person could describe. What particularly attracted Gould was that, because of his profession as an organizer and producer as well as seller of his books, he would, if he could get to be the first to examine these fresh species, be able to both describe and illustrate them. With such a wonderful commercial and scientific possibility, John Gould and his family landed in Tasmania in 1838. They (for his wife executed the illustrations) worked fast. The family soon moved to the mainland of Australia and by 1840 could return to England and, almost immediately, begin to publish the first parts of the books on Australian birds.

The demands for live Australian birds as zoological exhibits and household pets and stuffed ones to decorate glass cages and the hats of women can well be said to have begun with the publication of his books. Gould is credited with having been the first person to take live budgerigars out of Australia. Whether he also brought cockatiels back to England in 1840 is not known, but it is not unlikely, for their importation must have started at about this time as they were first bred in Europe in 1845.

Gould had named the cockatiel the "cockatoo-parrot," and by 1864 cockatoo-parrots were very well-known as pets for they were being brought back from Australia in quite considerable numbers. By far the most flourishing importer of exotic livestock into Britain at that time was a Mr. Jamrach, whose business continued to flourish, under his heirs, until the first world war (1914-1918) stopped it altogether. It was Mr. Jamrach, the founder, who coined the far more euphonious name of "cockatiel" for Gould's double-barrelled descriptive. Jamrach's choice of name was said to have come directly from the Dutch *kakatielje* which, in its turn, was said to have been directly derived from the Portugese for "little cockatoo," *cacatilho*.

The cockatiel by 1884 was extremely well-established as a breeding bird in European aviaries, and in English-speaking countries was now always known as the cockatiel. In 1902 David Seth-Smith wrote that the cockatiel was so well-known that a description seemed almost unnecessary, and that, except for the budgerigar, the cockatiel was, by far, the commonest Australian parrot in English aviaries where scores were being reared annually. He also said that four or more broods could be produced during the spring and summer and that a pair kept by him once reared sixteen youngsters between March and September.

Despite the ease with which the cockatiel had slipped into domestication, it is nevertheless probably true that until the Australian authorities forbade the export of native birds in 1960 further wild-caught ones still continued to be brought into Europe and America.

There is no reason why it should be supposed that the history of the cockatiel in North America was much different from that in Europe. Unfortunately documentation appears to be lacking. It does seem from the evidence, however, that the cockatiel has recently had far more popularity as a cage bird in America and South Africa than in Europe. Today, when there must be at least 10,000 of the new-colored cockatiels in Europe, the greater number of these are kept as aviary, and certainly not as cage, birds. And yet, strange as it must seem, before the introduction of the mutation colors, the cockatiel was never particularly common as an aviary bird. This does not mean that it was not well-known, but rather that many aviculturists, who are, it seems, always notoriously short of accommodations, preferred to house some-

The cockatiel is the smallest of the cockatoos; here an adult male cockatiel is shown in a size comparison with an adult greater sulphur-crested cockatoo. His gaze is directed admiringly—and possibly a little bit jealously—at the cockatoo's larger and more proudly carried crest. Photo by Louise van Der Meid.

24

what rarer parrots. Indeed the cockatiel was almost despised for being a "beginners' bird," a bird suitable for encouraging the novice in the hobby of bird-keeping because it bred so very easily. It was also a bird for the "pet-fancier" who had an aviary of budgerigars, canaries and cockatiels as a garden ornament. The cockatiel was typically the sort of bird that used to be put in aviaries in the parks of a city. On these grounds it is difficult not to believe that the total population of captive cockatiels, up to the late nineteen-sixties, may have been several times higher in the United States than in Europe, including Britain.

As the population of cockatiels in Europe, Africa and America had a rapid build-up in numbers after the last war, there must have been a considerable amount of inbreeding. It is inevitable that sooner or later in any large population of animals, and especially so in a group in which there is some individual inbreeding, a mutation will be hatched that radically differs in color from the general population.

The first recorded color mutation for the cockatiel happened in the U.S.A. and was piedness, although before then Mrs. E.L. Moon had been breeding light- and dark-colored grey cockatiels, some of which were said to be so light that they were almost white in color. The pieds, like most piebald animals, are at their most attractive when the pale areas are symmetrically placed making them neat and uniform in their pattern. Otherwise the pale areas so disrupt the normal appearance that they have a curious rather than an actually pleasing appearance.

Unfortunately, and this has happened with so many of the avian mutations, no one bothered to record its early history. Pieds, or harlequins as some term them, were already established before 1951. The next mutation, which was seemingly for cinnamon, took place in New Zealand, and in 1958 the first lutinos were hatched in Florida.

The phenomenal commerical success of the lutino and pied after they were imported into Europe opened the eyes of a good many bird breeders as to the scarcity and value of strangely colored parrots. The people who had pairs of these new colored cockatiels found that they were in a position to be able to, metaphorically, breed money. So great was the demand for these mutations that most breeders found that they needed a waiting list for prospective buyers. Some of the prices asked, and received, were stupendous. *Cockatiels had become big business!* It was perfectly possible that, by using well-tried normal cockatiels to incubate and raise the chicks, an owner of a fairly fertile pair of lutinos, in Europe at least, could, from 1960 to as late as 1970, make more money, tax-free, than he might have working for a wage. True, as the over-all number of these colored cockatiels increased, there was a diminishing return in their value, and the breeder might have needed to get twenty youngsters a year from a pair.

Strangely colored cockatiels might well have sometimes occurred before the arrival of the first lutino made people realize their commercial value. However, if such color mutations had previously happened they never persevered. But circumstances change events, and by the nineteen-sixties knowledgeable people actively sought to acquire any abnormally colored cockatiels they could find. The Dutch and the Belgians seem to have been most successful in this search. It was they who have largely developed the deep canary shade of the selected lutinos. They were also partly responsible for developing the "opaline" variety (which is more usually called the "pearled" or "laced") which had originated in West Germany in 1967. The cinnamon was found the next year in Belgium and the red-eyed or fallow the year after that.

By this time, however, the breeders had a much better understanding of genetics and had so perfected their management that now there was no comparison with the early history of the pied and lutino mutations which had taken years and years to become established in any quantity. Indeed, so fast was the increase in the numbers of these European-developed mutations that the market was rapidly overwhelmed by the numbers that they bred. The efficiency of the breeders caused the market for cockatiels to collapse by 1975 as far as astronomically high prices for any mutations were concerned. Indeed, it would have collapsed a few years earlier were it not that the South African government coinci-

These are two of the first lutino cockatiels ever produced in captivity. They formed part of the breeding stock from which all other lutino cockatiels sold in the bird trade have descended; they were bred by Cliff Barringer in Florida around 1958. Photo by Jay Jarrett.

Extending the wings to determine the amount of yellow coloration and the regularity of its dispersal throughout the feathering of a pied cockatiel. Photo by Miceli Studios.

dentally eased the restrictions on the importation of birds; the subsequent high importations conveniently emptied the birds from European aviaries.

In the search for novel mutations with an almost certain promise of financial gain, birds were stolen. The originator of the red-eyed silver is rumored to have lost his entire stock to thieves. At present the price of any of the color forms in Europe, when bought directly from the breeder, is roughly twice or, at most, three times the cost of a perfectly normally colored grey cockatiel. The exception is the fallow (the red-eyed silver), which retails at about ten times the value of a normal.

In several ways this money-making phase for the cockatiel has been extremely beneficial for aviculture. It has brought the breeding of captive parrots from a hit or miss affair to become practically a science. For the first time parrot breeders began to give thought to the nutrition of the parents and the chicks. They now sought to provide more suitable nest-boxes and tried to completely supervise the entire breeding cycle. Prior to this the invariable advice to breeders was that they must never interfere, whatever the circumstances, with nesting parrots because it might cause the parents to desert the chicks. However, the enormous difference in the quality and the number of young raised by these more scientific methods has even begun to convince the most traditional that there is considerably more to parrot breeding than a pair of birds, a nest-box and plenty of patience.

The Cockatiel as a
Pet Parrot

INTRODUCTION

The history of keeping parrots as pets is a long one. Practically all explorers on discovering a new tropical country have found that the natives kept tame parrots as household pets. The Amazon parrots, for example, that Christopher Columbus brought back to Spain from the New World were obtained, already tamed, from the Indians. Brazilian Indians to this day keep pet parrots and macaws, treasuring the shed feathers as ornamentation.

The first written account that parrots can imitate human speech comes from the ancient Greeks who, after Alexander the Great's conquests, obtained their parrots from India. They were very rare and later became almost mythical birds, until Roman explorers, during the reign of the Emperor Nero, discovered that Africa also had parrots. The trade of importing and training parrots to speak went on for hundreds of years, but no attempt seems to have been made by the Romans to breed them. It has been said that the Romans valued them so highly as pets that they were kept in cages made of tortoiseshell and ivory with silver wires. Once the Roman Empire fell into decay, it was not until the fifteenth century, the discovery of America and the exploration of the sea-routes to the Far East and beyond that parrots once more became known to the civilized world.

Yet, despite the ever-increasing trade between distant regions of the globe, parrots never really became available for any but the well-to-do or those fortunates who had sailor relatives until the introduction of the Australian parrots. Two species of these, the budgerigar and the cockatiel, were quite unlike parrots from elsewhere, for they bred most free-

The cockatiel's natural aloofness from human beings can be overcome if attempts at taming are made at the right time, during the
period in which the young bird is forming the patterns of behavior
that will guide it during the rest of its life. Photo by Louise van Der
Meid.

ly in captivity. Because they no longer had to be imported by
ship, they had cheapness and ready availability to recommend them. Nevertheless, it took surprisingly long before the
budgerigar began to oust the canary as a caged pet. By the
1930's the budgerigar was beginning to be very well known
as a talking bird and, at the time of writing, there must now
be thirty or forty of these parakeets for a single canary!

It has sometimes been suggested that the only way to get
a completely fearless parrot is to take it from the nest and
hand-rear it. This should not really be necessary as just as
equally tame pets can be made from youngsters that have
been reared by their parents *provided that they are taken
just after they have become self-supporting.* For all birds the
first few weeks after they leave the nest is a very important
period. This is when they learn how to adapt to their envir-

onment because they are then most mentally pliable. It is in these few days that birds can be tamed and taught to sample different foods and to pay attention to the sounds that they will later imitate. Once this brief period is over, further adaptions become increasingly more difficult and perhaps even impossible to accept.

It is perfectly natural for a young cockatiel to move away from non-bird-like animals. There are many instances where a perfectly tame, hand-reared young parrot has been put into an aviary and left very much alone. Within a couple of weeks it has become just as wild, indeed sometimes even wilder, than it would have been were it naturally reared. But if tame birds are kept in human company for several months then the tameness that they have will not usually desert them, even if they are then left very much alone.

BUYING A COCKATIEL

If the cockatiel is wanted as a pet it is very necessary that it be taken into the household when very young, otherwise it can be very difficult to completely tame. Although some mature birds may lose some of their wildness, there is only a very remote possibility that they will ever learn to talk. Wild birds never appear to be completely relaxed when confined to an occupied room, so the buyer must insist that he gets a youngster.

Should there be free choice, then the ideal youngster to get would be one that was already completely or partly tamed by hand-rearing or because it was taken early in life into close human companionship. Such a tame cockatiel could be easily picked out by being unconcerned, performing its natural functions such as eating and preening itself, when watched from close range.

Sick birds are apathetic and they should not be confused with tame ones! The lethargy of the sick is soon resumed after disturbance and the bird takes on a sleeping posture with its feathers fluffed around itself for extra warmth. Slight noises will arouse a healthy bird from its slumbers; the ill are less demonstrative. If the sick bird does feed, it will be done in a half-hearted way; nor will it be likely to groom it-

Healthy cockatiels usually *look* healthy, and sick cockatiels *look* sick, so it is important that you choose your pet from alert, active birds showing the glow of good condition. Photo by Harry V. Lacey.

self. It is extremely unwise to buy any bird that has the underside of the tail moist or caked with wet droppings, and avoid any that have a discharge from the nostrils or eyes. The strong probability in these cases is that the cockatiel may be ill with some disease and even though the possibility may be remote, it may be suffering with a disease such as salmonellosis or psittacosis that could be communicable to people. Infectious disease is comparatively rare in cockatiels; nevertheless those diseases that are found are more likely to affect youngsters than adult birds.

It is very difficult to give an exact age to youngsters and therefore the word of the vendor will have to be taken. This is especially so with the lutino, for in lutinos there is no known positive way for distinguishing adult hens from youngsters. We do have one very good guide for the other colors. The skin surrounding and composing the nostrils (the cere) is pink in fledglings and darkens to the adult grey-black in a few months. The cere of the lutino, however, is always flesh-pink irrespective of age. The cere of the red-eyed silver resembles that of the lutino. The feathers of normal cockatiels are much darker in the adult form than in youngsters, and this might also provide a clue as to birds' age.

Before buying the cockatiel, allow yourself sufficient time. Carefully examine the bird in a good light, first in the cage; later have it caught and feel its chest. A healthy bird moves with no trace of a limp, it has some weight, and the chest is firm and broad. And, please, never buy on an impulse! First make sure that the other members of the household also want a cockatiel's company.

When first brought home, re-examine it carefully after it has had a little while to settle down. Should it then appear to be ailing in some way or other do not delay before contacting the supplier of the bird. If several days are wasted before making the contact and the bird is then seriously ill the reply given may be that it would have been better to have known earlier for after a time all responsibility has ended. Fortunately, almost all cases of seeming illness will prove to be dejection. The slight shock inevitably resulting from the stress of capture and transportation will be fully gone after a

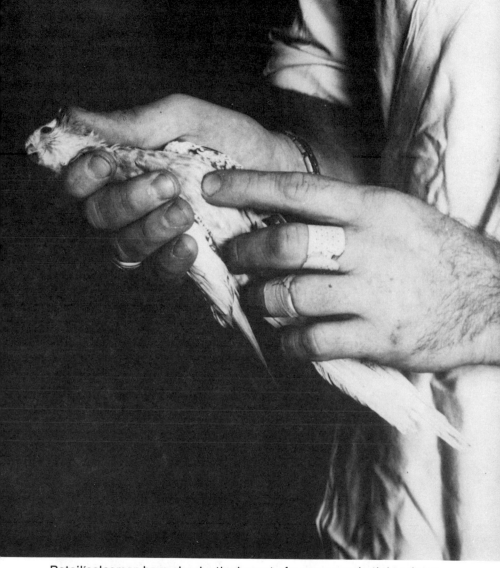

Retail salesman here checks the breast of a young cockatiel to determine its fullness. The chest should have a roundness and plumpness to it, and the breastbone should not stick out sharply. Photo by Miceli Studios.

day in the cage. Nevertheless, it might be welcome in some cases to have the dealer's opinion on the matter.

It is far better not to put an animal of any description into an entirely strange cage or aviary if it will not have a few hours in which to settle down before nightfall. It will prove far less damaging to the young cockatiel's nervous system if, should it not arrive until near dusk, it be held overnight in the traveling box until the morning so that it can have a whole day in which to accustom itself to its surroundings, find its food and water and select a perch on which to roost for the night.

THE CAGE

In the wild the cockatiel may find its food by walking over the surface of the ground looking for seeds. Some days it must walk considerable distances in this search, for the food is most likely to be widely scattered. Cockatiels can climb like other parrots, using their beak as a third hand, among twigs and branches, but they cannot manage this with any great efficiency. Nor need they when so small a proportion of their diet comes from trees. These behavioral patterns suggest that the floor of the cage is as important, or perhaps even more important, than the number of perches or the height. The very tall cylindrical cages sometimes seen have little to recommend them for cockatiels. An ideal cage would, of course, be large enough for the bird to actually be able to fly from one perch to another. But this is impractical because such a four-foot-long or even longer cage would be hard to fit into the average room, therefore with the usual small cage the bird is best allowed out for a daily walk and fly-around—*after it is tamed!*

Most pet cockatiels will be housed in all-metal or plastic and metal cages that are primarily designed with the budgerigar in mind. However, such a parakeet cage is actually far too confining. Unfortunately most of the larger cages one can buy are really intended for the bigger perching parrots and have generally been made to a design that has shown little modification in the past hundred years. Several other cages are only too obviously made to be an ornament first with

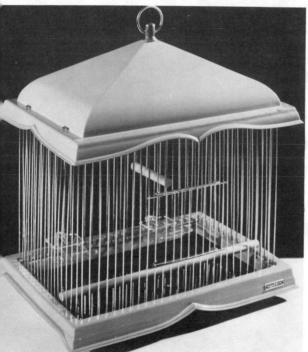

Bird cages come in many different styles and sizes, but not every cage is suitable for use as cockatiel housing. Ask your dealer for specific recommendations about which type of cage should be purchased.

little thought given to the needs of the bird. A cage should be at least reasonably strongly put together and needs no superfluous ornamentation. There can often be considerable beauty in simplicity of construction, and in practice a flat-topped oblong cage takes a lot of beating. This oblong shape wastes no internal space and allows for any side of the cage to be placed flat against a vertical surface; most usefully, objects put on the top of the cage cannot slip to the ground. Your petshop will be able to recommend a proper cage providing they are specialists in birds and not a dime-store operation which is usually poorly staffed and probably even more poorly stocked.

Cockatiels are natural acrobats and should be given enough cage-room to indulge themselves in activities that provide them with needed exercise. Photo by Miceli Studios.

A tall rectangular cage with good-size base dimensions provides a fairly large exercise area for birds kept indoors; one big advantage of a cage of such design is that it can be placed in a corner in the bird room without wasting any space. Photo by Louise van Der Meid.

TAMING

There are those who suggest that taming should begin immediately with the purchase of the bird. Their case is a strong one, for these early days are so important in the taming process; while the bird is distracted with its new surroundings, it will be made all the easier to familiarize it with human contact. Yet, the more especially if the bird has traveled a long way, it might be allowed a full day in which to accustom itself to its new environment and to find the location of its food and water. For the cockatiel's short life, prior to its purchase, must have been one of continual change and now it has met another. A month or less before purchase its world was the interior of a nest-box and the only living things with which it was acquainted were its several brothers and sisters and its parents. Once it left the nest it most likely spent the next two or three weeks in the aviary with its parents while it learned about wire-netting, how to fly, to land and how to feed and drink for itself. It was probably now that it made its first acquaintance with human beings. After a frightening chase it must have been caught in a net and taken to the dealer's premises for its short stay. Overall it would have been subject to many frights and upsets and now, for the first time, it is kept in isolation from other cockatiels in another set of unfamiliar surroundings.

Young animals are extremely adaptable; they have to be. None of these early frightening experiences should have damaged it mentally or physically. It may have an odd broken feather which will molt out in a few months' time and frights may be forgotten. In its new cage everything is likely to be completely strange, even, perhaps, the way that the seed is fed from small raised containers. The cockatiel may not recognize these small dishes as being a source of food. To make it easier for it to do so, some of the seed should be scattered onto the floor of the cage and the container itself be overfilled so that the seed is brought into full view. The seed provided should be of the widest possible mixture so that at least some will be of the same type to which it had been previously accustomed. For the first day water may also be provided from a small heavy container to stop its being spilt.

When it is first seen that the cockatiel stands on his perches and eats and drinks from the correct containers, which is usually by the second day, the floor of the cage can be cleaned of the loose seed and the water dish.

The cage is best placed on a firm table. A frightened cockatiel always flies up from the ground, and if the table is high it must give the bird a greater feeling of security. If for the first day the top and back of the cage are covered with a towel, the partial seclusion this gives might allow the bird to relax better and it might also encourage the bird to eat. The main periods for eating are shortly after rising and again in the evening when the light is poorer; the towel-dimmed light might serve the same function. If the bird has not eaten after a day, try offering a millet spray; if that fails to start it to eat, please contact the person who sold the cockatiel. But as grain-eating birds such as these can easily withstand starvation for a day or two, there should be no need to panic.

Once the bird is seen to eat and drink, taming had better not be deferred: *remember that the adaptability of the young is increasingly lost to age.*

A young cockatiel taken away from the companionship of its parents and siblings and injected into a strange new environment will be under considerable stress, but if it is given sensible care it will soon adapt. Photo by Louise van Der Meid.

Basically, there are two methods of taming. The first, even if it is the one favored by the author, may not always give a completely tame bird unless considerable free time is available daily. It does take longer, but its simplicity lies in that the cockatiel becomes tame largely by its own unconscious effort. The second well-tried method was first explained by Russ and has been recommended as the method of choice by Bates and Busenbark in their *Parrots and Related Birds*. It is far, far quicker and in principle is similar to the standard way of training a hawk to the wrist.

The first method uses a much slower process of habituation. The cockatiel must be kept in a place where there is some continual movement or noise, such as in a well used room. For the first day the cockatiel may be ignored save to notice that sooner or later it will have become sufficiently settled to crack seed and, perhaps, preen itself. As it eats it will stop as a sudden noise or movement takes its attention, then, after a pause, begin once again. After a few repetitions the sounds and the distractions of the room that stopped its feeding will cease to attract its attention. By the second day the cockatiel should be familiar enough with the normal activity around it not to mind being closely watched by someone who should try talking to the bird in a low soothing voice. Such quiet noises help to settle wild animals, for in nature loud noises usually signify alarm and so does an absolute silence: the lull, the quiet moment of indecision before the predator makes its sudden grabbing movement. In the beginning, when near the cage all movements, such as changing the water or food, should be made slowly. If the cockatiel begins to panic any movement should be stopped and the bird talked to in a quiet soothing way until it has quieted once more. By the second or third day the hand, which has until then been held only to the front of the cage, can be moved toward the bird when it preens itself in an attempt to scratch the top is its head with a finger. A person who is particularly worried about getting nipped by the bill may use a twig or a dull-colored pencil. To get the bird nearer to the front of the cage a slice of apple or millet spray or, best of all, a few heads of some seeding grass or an annual weed

42

Regardless of which of the two basic methods of taming a cockatiel is used, the object of the taming process is to make the bird unafraid of contact with its owner so that it will readily perch on a finger and can easily be removed from or returned to its cage. These obviously well-tamed cockatiels were trained by their owner, Teena Cummings, shown with them here. Photo by Dr. Herbert R. Axelrod.

pushed through the bars usually brings it forward to feed. Because cockatiels are very nervous at settling on leafy branches, it is best to give a little green food at a time in case a larger bunch frightens it.

Head preening is such a very important aspect of a cockatiel's social behavior that once the bird accepts the familiarity of having its head scratched it can be said to be all but tamed. During the first few attempts to stroke the top of the head the bird may make a few feints with the bill, but it is extremely unlikely that it will actually bite. Young birds cannot and do not bite as viciously as do adults.

As much time as is conveniently possible ought to be spent close to the bird. To make this easier the cage can be moved about so that almost all the household chores are performed with the bird as an audience. If the youngster was rather unfamiliar with human beings when first acquired, it would have rocked from side to side as it squatted on the floor of the cage and hissed angrily through its open beak. This display of fright and intimidation is usually lost within a few hours, never to return.

The next stage, which is to get the bird to perch on a finger, can also precede the attempts to scratch its head. To do this the hand is introduced through the opened door of the cage with the index finger leading. As always, avoid alarming the bird by speaking softly and moving with extreme caution. If the cockatiel becomes tense stop the movement, but as it relaxes move the hand further forward, keeping it below the bird until the edge of the index finger is pressed lightly against the lower part of the bird's chest just above its feet. With the finger held so close, it becomes rather uncomfortable for the bird to maintain this posture and, therefore, it should step upon the finger. If the finger is held higher than this then the cockatiel, before it steps on, may take a slight hold with the open beak. As this is not intended to be a bite, and is little more than a means of steadying the body while it makes a step forward, the finger ought not to be pulled away and so needlessly startle the bird. Once the cockatiel is perched on the finger the hand should be held steady long enough for the cockatiel to become fully compos-

The hand must be inserted into the cage slowly so as not to alarm the cockatiel. At the first sign of fright by the bird, the trainer should stop the movement of the hand and wait until the bird is once again composed; movement of the hand should then *slowly* be resumed. Photo by Dr. Herbert R. Axelrod.

ed. After the bird has relaxed for a little while the hand can be moved slowly toward whichever perch the cockatiel faces to make the perch press lightly against its lower chest. Then, as before with the finger, it should step upon the perch.

Once this has been done several times and after making fully certain that all doors and windows are closed and that no animals (this includes small children) are left in the room (the most seemingly placid dog or cat can move with surprising swiftness to pounce upon a fluttering bird), get the cockatiel to perch on a finger, as before, and take your hand cautiously from the cage. Once the bird is outside, try to scratch its head with the other hand or give it a little millet spray or a few pieces of hand-held grasses to nibble, things to relax the bird and subdue its fears. It is perhaps best if the cockatiel is not kept out of the cage for too long before being

45

returned. However, after a few such short trips, instead of returning it to the perch inside the cage allow it to step onto the top of the cage and, as before, generally fuss a bit to distract it in its first spell of freedom from the cage and hand.

At about this time, when putting the bird back into its cage by the usual method of transportation on a finger, the other hand can be used to lightly envelop the bird with the fingers placed ever so gently around its body, tightly enough to prevent its escape but loosely enough not to make it feel constrained. By this method it can be carried anywhere. With much repetition the cockatiel will lose all fear of this contact and may then always be picked up without any struggle. There is often a temptation to walk out-of-doors with a tame, full-winged parrot perched on a shoulder. Unfortunately no matter how tame the bird or how usually obedient to calls, sooner or later it will get frightened by some sudden movement and once on the wing could easily disappear and be lost forever. Never take a cockatiel outside unless its wing is clipped.

During the early training the cockatiel may become startled and fly off around the room to land awkwardly somewhere. In the early stages of training it is best to pick the bird up by making it climb onto a finger pressed lightly against its chest and, if necessary, by cupping the other hand around its body for extra security. When any bird takes flight in a room, never chase it. It must land. After it does so, cautiously approach it with the minimum of delay, before it gets its senses, and get it to stand on a finger. Until the cockatiel gets to know the geography of the room, the drapes might be better pulled to prevent it bruising itself from flying into the glass. From now on it can be let out of the cage at all times. The more time that is spent in the beginning with the bird, and the more gentle the handling, the quicker will it become confiding.

The inexperienced bird trainer tends to fear getting bitten. But because young cockatiels never bite unless they are badly frightened by being held, this fear will go. Training can take place if another caged bird is in the room, but progress is much quicker without this distraction.

The second method is quicker by far. It has been said that it takes only part of a day to subdue a young parrot into tameness; this I do not doubt. The method depends upon giving an unremitting, continuous stimulation to the senses of contact, sight and sound at the same time preventing the cockatiel from escaping. Under this continual stress the parrot's nervous system eventually ceases to respond. It rapidly becomes indifferent, or inured, to what previously were frightening stimuli. This process of rapid habituation appears to be largely irreversible and the bird, once tamed, remains so. In the above summary I have tried to avoid the term "brain-washing," but it is too apt to be passed over.

A near-essential for this second method is to make the bird flightless, for by doing so a considerable amount of chasing about will be avoided. The more usual method of stopping a bird from flying is to cut the flight feathers from ONE wing with a pair of scissors. To do this someone has to hold the bird with its wing outstretched while another person snips the feathers off. If the scissors are held parallel to the leading edge of the wing, leaving behind about an inch of quill, the flight feathers can be removed with one snip. For the fainthearted it should be remembered that the feathers, except when they are growing and in "pin," are, like hair, technically dead structures and are therefore insensitive to pain. Obviously special care must be taken not to cut the bird's flesh. Because the bird can have its flight restored after it has been tamed, the kinder method is to stick the flight feathers, again of one wing only, in a resting position by using two strips of adhesive tape. One strip goes under the wing and one over. Very little tape is required although some help will be needed to apply it. This frail structure is sufficient to stop the bird from using the wing because the muscles that extend the wing are not particularly strong. Yet with a wing so bound the bird ought to be even less able to fly than one with cut feathers. Strip the tape off when it is no longer needed.

The cockatiel, unable to fly with its impaired wing, is taken in the hand. Some may prefer to use a glove, but it is far more difficult to assess the pressure put upon the bird

During the "intensive" method of taming a cockatiel—subjecting it to a constant handling to break down its natural reserve quickly— the bird must be deprived of its capacity for flight by having one wing clipped or taped. The bird shown here has been wing-clip- ped. Photo by Dr. Herbert R. Axelrod.

Two different types of wing clips, showing the pattern of feathers remaining in each case.

through the thickness of the glove than with a bare hand. Remember that boa constrictors and pythons kill their prey by holding them just tight enough in their coils to stop any chest movements and so asphyxiate them. The trainer holds the bird fairly low down and slowly relaxes his hold. The cockatiel will usually, on finding itself free, perch for an instant on the fingers and then try to fly off. But, because it is pinioned, it will flutter to the ground instead. As it lands it should be immediately encircled with the ungloved hands held with the palms facing upward and the fingers making a basket shape. To escape now the cockatiel has to climb forward and up over the fingers to perch on the uppermost ones before it can attempt to fly off. It will not bite but, as mentioned earlier, a parrot climbing onto something somewhat higher than its feet often takes a steadying "first step" with its beak. There is, therefore, no reason to be alarmed if the landed cockatiel puts out its head toward the encircling

Lifting the wing-clipped cockatiel from the floor must be done slowly to avoid unduly frightening the bird; often it will of its own accord
hop onto the back of a hand outstretched to corral it. If it jumps off
the hand while the hand is being raised, the capturing process
should be repeated—slowly and gently does the trick. Photo by
Connie Allen.

With the bird perched on one finger, the index finger of the other hand is slowly brought into contact with the bird's chest, creating in the bird a need to climb onto the finger gently pressing against its chest. Photo by Connie Allen.

fingers, for it is not intending to bite. You will have to repeat this again and again until the cockatiel begins to settle for a while on the fingers before tumbling forward. However, once it does begin to pause for a while the method changes and the bird is now to be lifted up by pressing an index finger against its lower chest. As it steps onto the finger the index finger of the opposite hand is now similarly pressed against its lower chest and it will climb onto this. The original finger is now moved forward again to make it step once again onto this and so on. The movement from the index finger of one hand to the index finger of the other should be made continual so the bird moves as if it were climbing up a never-ending set of stairs. But as the hands are simultaneously being lowered the cockatiel actually remains in the same approximate position in space, just above the floor. As with all training, talk to it continuously.

This photo illustrates the basic "step-climbing" operation to which the bird must become accustomed. As it moves onto the finger touching its chest, the other index finger is brought into contact with the bird's chest. The actions are repeated until the finger-hopping becomes automatic. Photo by Dr. Herbert R. Axelrod.

The bird will be noticed to become increasingly reluctant to move at the rate which is being set by the moving fingers and it will, at some point, stop altogether. In this case a slight tap with the presenting finger should set it off again. This first hesitancy is a true indication that the cockatiel is becoming tame. It is demonstrating that it is becoming accustomed to human contact by the relaxation of its nervous state. Shortly it will be steady enough to permit a gentle caressing of its head. Two hours or so from starting, the cockatiel, provided that it was a young bird, should be completely tame. The best result will be obtained if one person only does the training. For the next week or two get the bird onto the hand sometime during the day, taking it straight from the cage and spending some time scratching its head. Within a week its tameness should be irreversible, provided that human contact is maintained.

THE PET OF THE HOUSEHOLD

Tame cockatiels are usually so very affectionate that it is rather cruel, as well as unnecessary, to confine them only to the small world that is their cage. The health of all parrots is bettered when they are allowed to come out of the cage for exercise, and it also allows them to make contact with people rather than have people always approach the bird. Try calling gently to the bird whenever it is given a tidbit. After many times it should associate this noise with food and it will be most useful, more especially if the bird ever accidently escapes, to call it back again. When the bird is regularly let out of its cage it will be noticed that it does not make full use of the room but prefers only certain places to walk and perch. A little ingenuity on the part of the owner can modify these favored places so that it can do very little damage with its beak and create less nuisance from its droppings.

Certain people who have a wide experience with the larger climbing parrots sometimes say that the cockatiel is rather a stupid bird compared with these others. This is not necessarily so. The behavior modifications needed for ground-feeding are much simpler than those that are needed by a tree-feeding, that is a climbing, parrot. Even the tamest

Once it is finger-tamed a cockatiel should be allowed free flight outside its cage so that it can obtain needed exercise. Cockatiels allowed such free flight usually have favorite perching spots in the room housing their cage. Photo by Dr. Herbert R. Axelrod.

cockatiel is, at some point, quite likely to severely panic and rapidly take flight upward in a frantic attempt to get as far away from whatever it was that frightened it in the shortest time possible. Because the usual green-colored parrot is reasonably safely hidden by its camouflage of color as it clambers among the branches of trees, it is their practice to keep perfectly still. This pause before taking action gives the climbing parrots time to "consider" what to do next. The cockatiel, searching the ground for seed often considerably well away from the protection of bushes or trees, has only one safe place to go when alarmed, and that is into the air and away. This "safety device" is too instinctive to be affected by captivity.

The majority of parrots can hold things in a foot, which they use as a hand, and, although very many cockatiels have been closely studied, only one has been seen that could do this. The lack of this ability has resulted because the natural food of the cockatiel is small seeds which never need any steadying with the foot. Indeed, the bird picks these up from the ground and shells them at such an extraordinarily fast rate that if the foot had to be used it would slow their eating rate down quite considerably. These and the other differences between cockatiels and climbing parrots are therefore not proofs of stupidity but simply reflections of a natural selection for an entirely different way of life.

Except when they nest, cockatiels seldom bathe in standing water but they do particularly love to be showered by falling spray or rain. If a tame cockatiel can find its way into the kitchen or bathroom and can hear and see a running faucet, it will most likely attempt to shower underneath. Once it learns to do this it may be unlucky enough at one time or another to steal a bath when the water is hot and so be tragically killed. It is therefore better not to teach them this trick but to buy a small spray sold specifically for this purpose or to use a child's watering can with a fine "rose" attachment. The cockatiel can be made to stand on an absorbent towel for its shower. As a cockatiel takes its bath it will usually stretch itself and squeal with delight as it thoroughly wets every part of its body.

A parrot putting its zygodactyl foot to food use in holding a piece of watermelon. Although cockatiels have zygodactyl feet, they aren't as adept as parrots in using them for holding things and for climbing.

Sometimes one hears the opinion that it is wrong to teach a domesticated animal tricks. It is difficult to follow this train of thought: a dog that comes when called or sits or lies on a word of command is a distinct improvement on one that is not house-trained and is willfully independent. A captive parrot can have a very boring existence. However, if it is regularly taught tricks not only would it be less bored but it becomes interesting to the owner. It is only possible to teach an animal to do things that are within its capabilities, and the things that a cockatiel does well are to pull or push with the beak, to get into dark holes, and to climb and walk. A cockatiel can be taught to open things with the beak, to turn handles, to open and close small doors, and to work small mills with the feet or beak. Any amount of ingenuity can be used to make various developments upon these basic ideas.

TEACHING TO TALK

Although an extremely wide group of birds is known to be able to mimic sounds, the parrots excel at this. Indeed, practically the first question asked by visitors, and especially children, to anyone with a parrot is "Does he talk?". From the evidence it does appear that all species of parrot have this facility even if individuals differ widely in their final attainment.

The budgerigar seems to have a better memory for prolonged phrases of sound than any other parrot. One called "Sparky Williams" had a particularly retentive memory and can be heard on a commercial record (Phillips BL 7824) by Phillip Marsden called "Talking Budgerigars" repeating many complete nursery rhymes, practically faultlessly, as well as chattering endearments and odd scraps of nonsense.

The size of the parrot is important in determining the finished pitch of the voice it reproduces, although size may make little difference as to clarity. The average African grey parrot could not acquire anything like the extensive repertoire of the average budgerigar, but the grey parrot would have a much greater fidelity to the original. The very best of talking budgerigars usually say their words in a hoarse-sounding, whispering, chattering way and usually very careful attention has to be given before catching exactly what it is repeating. Indeed, as with very young children, it is often only after it has been interpreted by someone familiar with its words that one can make out exactly what is being said.

Even if the cockatiel repeats its words with far more clarity than the budgerigar, its voice still has a rather "reedy" quality which makes it sound not unlike a child with a slight cold in the head. Cockatiels do not usually pick up a large vocabulary of words, but they are very capable of whistling tunes. In general, and allowing for individual variation, male parrots are far and away superior to females in their talking ability. This might well be because hens have a naturally more restricted vocabulary, for they are altogether quieter. Most of the sounds that hen parrots make are not learned but come naturally. Such "inherited" sounds give warning of danger, attract the attention of others or yield other simple information. Irrespective of species, the majority of male parrots have two songs. The first is definitely sexual. It is given as a challenge to other males or is directed at the female to stimulate her into reproductive activity. Most of such songs are innate, but portions can be learned or modified. The second form of song is usually much quieter and is heard usually when the bird is relaxed and settled. It consists of a series of chattering or whistling sounds. Some hens also have this relaxed, twittering "private" song; although some phrases of it are innate, whole passages can be learned.

Lastly there are noises that the bird makes to draw attention to itself and, being directed towards itself, they are mostly learned. Much of the "conversation" of parrots is of this latter kind: "pretty Joey," "Polly wants a kiss," etc. But the most interesting passages can be heard in the true courtship song. This is the twittering speaking of the budgerigar. The most remarkable imitations are often heard in the self-amusing private song. Examples may be given. The author has a spectacled Amazon, *Amazona albifrons*, that draws attention to itself not only by its "natural" cries but by calling "Enrico, Bueno Enrico" and if someone laughs it will immediately "laugh" back. But it will seldom give its laugh at an imitation laugh; it has to be the real thing. The courtship song of this bird is a mixture of all its repertoire, but its "private" song is given only when it is completely relaxed and most usually if music is being played on the radio. Then it laughs like a tiny, tickled human baby and the baby cries and baby-talks and coughs. These sounds of a very, very tiny child are wonderfully accurate, but I know of no way of getting the parrot to do this except when it is quiet and still and seemingly resting.

Teaching a parrot to talk is much more complicated than merely repeating a phrase over and over again as it will eventually only imitate those noises that have caught its interest. A woman's voice is much easier for a parrot to learn and a whistled tune is easier than a phrase. Because it is so invariably taught, a "wolf-whistle" must be one of the easiest of noises for a parrot to make. It is, however, to myself—a mere male—an extremely infuriating noise at its thousandth repetition and more. Perhaps more thought ought to be given to what is to be taught to a parrot. It is best to select something very simple such as "Hellow" followed by the bird's name. By making skillful use of two tape recorders it is simple to make a continuous tape consisting of the same identical words by first recording the short phrase on one and then using this original to put a series of identicals on the second. Such a tape can be played when no one is in the room. The trouble with this method is that the cockatiel may learn it as a continuous phrase. Instead of repeating "pretty Joey," or what-have-you, it says instead "Joey pretty Joey pretty Joey...." *ad infinitum.*

Once the first phrase has been mastered, continue to teach the bird. Parrots are very unlike the extremely talented Indian hill mynahs which learn, with a remarkable facility, a most extensive repertoire and yet stop increasing their vocabulary after their first year. Parrots can learn new words and sounds for many, many years.

It is, on the face of it, extremely strange why certain birds should be able to imitate the sound of the human voice. The voice of a human being is produced by the vocal cords, aided by the movement of tongue and lips, changing

Mynah birds are more facile than cockatiels in learning how to talk, but the period during which they can learn new sounds is much shorter than the cockatiel's learning period. Photo by Dr. Herbert R. Axelrod.

Parrot species with a reputation for being good talkers (such as the African grey parrot, right) are generally superior to most other birds (including cockatiels and budgies) in the *quality* of their reproduced sounds but not necessarily in the extent of their vocabulary. Photo by Horst Mueller.

the shape of our mouth cavity, and by altering the force with which we expel air from our lungs. A ventriloquist gets our wonder by the amazing way that he is able to produce the consonants B,F,M,P,V, and W without using his lips. One might think that a bird would have far more difficulty than the ventriloquist who has, after all, only to substitute the "fricative sounds" by some ingenuity of pronunciation. It can be easily shown that the tongue of the parrot plays no part in forming any of the sounds it makes by watching its movements inside the beak of a talking parrot. The traditional advice to cut a bird's tongue before teaching it to speak, by using two silver coins working together like a pair of scissors, was believed to give a "silver tongue" by "freeing its movement." This is senseless, cruel nonsense. It can do nothing but harm to the parrot, as it must make eating difficult, for the tongue is needed to steady the food that is shelled by the beak.

The parrot likewise has neither lips, cheeks nor vocal cords. However, it does have a very effective sound-box, the syrinx, at the base of the windpipe. It is believed that most sounds originate here. Mammals have precisely the same vocal apparatus as humans and yet they have little or no ability to reproduce sounds foreign to their species. It is true that a few individual chimpanzees have been laboriously taught to make such simple sounds as "cup" or "mom" but no chimpanzee has managed an even slightly more difficult word nor has it linked two or three words into a simple phrase. The problem is not only *how* do birds make sounds, but *why* do they imitate?

In general, birds make far more complex noises than mammals and the more intricate the sounds they make the more likely it is that some will be mimicry. The remainder of the song or call is inherent. The innate sounds are somewhat basic and perform such functions as warning of danger, threatening another bird, and bringing wandering chicks back to the hen. But even the innate sounds can be greatly modified by imitation.

It almost invariably is written that parrots do not use their facility for mimicry in the wild, not that this dogmatic statement is ever substantiated by fact. Certainly it would be extraordinary if the parrots kept such an undoubted talent permanently unused. Otherwise why should they have it so well-developed? Indeed, pairs of captive parrots inevitably learn to reproduce the sounds they hear from their immediate background. Still more impressively, they particularly learn to imitate each other. The author has a male African grey parrot who loudly says "Good morning Joe," and now so does his "wife" and all his offspring. The family also wolf-

Cockatiels will repeat sounds learned from each other and from other bird species more readily than they will learn to repeat the sounds their owners want them to make, so it is best that birds being taught to talk be maintained outside the presence of other birds during the training process. Photo by Manolo Guevara.

whistle and repeat various phrases and a small dog barking. These are sounds that the male first learned several years ago when as a caged pet he was kept in isolation from his own kind. He may well not have heard except from his "wife"— and she learned them from him—these noises in the original since.

This might show that a pair of parrots, and perhaps the small flock to which they belong, have a common "vocabulary" which completely identifies them from other parrots. The courtship call and warble of a male cockatiel is a very simple series of noises and yet, even if they are much alike, it is easy to say exactly, once one knows one's birds, which particular male is calling. And if we can do this, presumably their "wives" similarly can. It appears that parrots are more ready to accept sounds for reproduction from one of themselves rather than from the background. That is, they are more likely to reproduce another parrot's talking than they are a human being's. It seems logical to assume that the common sounds that members of a pair share become a code of recognition, in the same way that an ewe recognizes its lamb at a distance by its voice. The parrot might thus identify its flock or its partner, even though they may be completely hidden by the foliage or intermingled with a larger flock of strange parrots. If so, the sound code between a pair may help to cement the pair bond by a system of sounds that mean absolutely nothing to any other animal or bird.

If this hypothesis has any truth it would demonstrate that it would be much easier for a parrot to learn to talk when it is kept in complete isolation from its own kind. This we know is true. It will also be easier for a parrot to learn from someone to whom it is deeply attached. As talking and imitation in general often take place when the bird is resting and relaxed, such occasions might be the best time to teach them to talk.

The Wild Cockatiel

(The major portion of the material for this chapter has come from a thesis by Richard Zann and an article in Avicultural Magazine. *See* **Bibliography**.)

Although no one yet appears to have provided the necessary study figures, it does seem that, in terms of their population, the commonest of the wild Australian parrots are the budgerigar and the cockatiel. Both these can be found in very small numbers in what is virtually desert and in slightly larger numbers although still scarce, in semi-desert, the mallee (a type of scrub desert), and permanent pastures. The largest populations are to be found in the temporary grasslands and open savannah. Over this wide distribution the cockatiel nowhere appears to reach the coast nor has it been recorded from heavily timbered country. This range of possible habitats makes the total area of Australia that they might inhabit very large indeed, comparing in total area with the area of the United States and that of Europe. Yet they are very much dependent on the vagaries of rainfall, as most of this area is subject to drought, and they are consequently very unevenly distributed over this large territory.

In their streamlined shape they are most unlike the more sedentary parrot species. They have the wing structure, long tail and well-developed flight muscles to enable them to fly the considerable distances that sometimes are necessary as they travel in search of seeds and water in these often very arid areas. They are largely nomadic, staying in one area until the food supply runs out, which frequently is a matter of days. In some parts of their range, because of a more regular weather pattern, the movements of the cockatiel will take approximately the same annual course and they then appear to be migratory. In general, however, their wander-

64

The younger the baby cockatiel becomes accustomed to human handling, the easier the bird will be to train. Owners who hand-feed their baby cockatiels are looked upon by their birds with almost the same degree of trust that the babies would give their own parents. Photo by Dr. Gerald R. Allen.

ings are almost random. This is perfectly demonstrated by the fact that the consequent intermingling of populations has prevented the cockatiel from forming any distinct geographical races. The whole population looks very much alike.

They largely depend for food on the small sun-dried seeds that fall from vegetation that grows in otherwise barren areas following very heavy rainfall. This greenery soon comes to a rapid fruition and then wilts and dies. Cockatiels are certainly able to live for a long time without water provided that they do not have to fly far or exert themselves in any great way. For this would cause them to have to pant off water vapor to cool themselves. The moisture they must have for their body when they are deprived of drinking water comes from metabolizing the seed.

The interior of Australia can provide a very harsh existence as, to a large degree, the rains are neither predictable nor regular. Indeed some large portions of the continent can go for years without any appreciable moisture falling, even though the *average* interval between heavy rains may be measured in months. In years of prolonged drought tremendous numbers of cockatiels and other desert-specialized birds, including budgerigars, must die from thirst and starvation.

It must happen, in what are otherwise extremely barren areas, that enough rain will fall to grow a reasonably good crop of seeds and so provide food for a long time. When this fortunate happening occurs the cockatiels are able to remain long enough to breed. But it has to be a race against time before the crop becomes exhausted. Of course, not only the cockatiels take advantage of such a situation. Other birds, both the nomadic ones, such as other species of cockatoo, the budgerigar, finches and doves, and the largely resident ones will also move into the area together with rodents, marsupials, seed-eating ants and other insects. Because of the overall importance of time, the eggs of the cockatiel have to be laid in as brief a span of time as possible after the "decision" to breed has been made. Likewise the incubation and rearing time are best contracted to a minimum. If time can be saved the parents can possibly rear other broods while the food lasts. Consequently natural selection has shortened the breeding cycle. In theory if the rains continue to fall frequently and the crop of seeds is thereby constantly replenished, the parents may be able to breed continuously. In practice this would not be possible. A more residential type of parrot would begin to populate and, by competition, oust the cockatiel.

The rain upon which their breeding is ultimately dependent may be neither restricted to a definite season of the year nor, in the terrain in which they live, can it always be an annual event. Therefore the mystery is: how can the cockatiels have an inkling as to when a favorable germinating and growing period for the transient vegetation is likely to come? What stimulus is it that sets them breeding? Prior to the chicks hatching the food supply might, within reason, not particularly matter. Egg-laying requires, perhaps, very little extra food. This is because in hen cockatiels the yolk (ova) of the egg is, from the evidence of post-mortem examinations, seemingly mostly present in mature hens. Long before she lays, yolks are continually being developed and resorbed. It seems most unlikely that the stimulus to breed is provided by a sudden upsurge in the quality or the amount of food because, unless they usually live in a state of near-starvation, the amount of food eaten each day must, in the nature of things, often vary in amount. Nor can it be the amount of water that is available, for it is easy to imagine a permanent and readily available source of water that lies within an otherwise arid area. The need is for the cockatiels to arrange their breeding cycle so that sufficient food is available when the chicks hatch and to continue until they become self-supporting. That is from about a month onward from the time that the parents have first decided on their nesting cavity, and then for another two months.

The breeding cycle seems likely to be triggered by the onset of rainy weather. When a thick black rain cloud moves over the face of the sun and it suddenly becomes dark, cockatiels become excited and call to each other in a wild way as they fly from perch to perch. On landing they spread their wings fully out by their sides, with the tail fanned

The weather has an effect on how much a cockatiel will drink just as it has an effect on how much other animals will drink; birds maintained outdoors during warm weather normally will make more trips to the water dish than birds kept indoors. Photo by Dr. Gerald R. Allen.

Opposite:
The cockatiel doesn't have the brilliancy of coloration of most of the other parrots, but it has a subdued beauty all its own and is a very attractive bird in its own right. Photo by Dr. Gerald R. Allen.

open. In this outstretched position they teeter forward to hang almost vertically downward from the perch. Sometimes the self-same inverted display is done hanging from or near the entrance hole of the nest chamber after the bird comes from the darkness inside into the brightness of the day. Sometimes caged cockatiels similarly suspend themselves with wings and tail flared when a light is turned on.

As rain starts to fall, and most especially after a dry spell, the cockatiel will fly around in an ecstasy of excitement, giving their flight call of *weel, weel*. They perch with the wings and tail spread wide to catch the falling drops and hang upside down to wet the few remaining dry areas of the body. This fluttering and posturing and shrieking has all the wild, excited abandon of young children who, out of sight of the parents, have found for themselves a nice muddy puddle to splash in. Once the cockatiels are sopping wet they sit drying and preen themselves and their partners' heads. The excitement of flying and posturing usually sets off the males into a frenzy of sexual display. They sing to their hens and give the *wher-wetit whew* and *were-it, were-it, were-it* calls. The calling begins slowly and gradually increases to a tempo. The male also starts to search for nesting holes, accompanied by his "wife." If the rain continues long enough this daily activity starts the pair nesting in earnest.

It seems that adult cockatiels remain paired throughout most of the year. When the opportunity to breed does come they do not have to frantically search for a mate and then undertake a rapid courtship. The permanent bond between a mated pair is strengthened not only by mutal head-preening and close attendance one upon the other, but also by copulation. Pairing may take place several times a day except for when they are molting. The hen can lay fertile eggs within about four days of the pair finding a suitable cavity in which to lay, the ovaries being in a state of full development for most of the year.

Due to storm damage and drought many of the trees of inland Australia have some, or several, dead limbs. The center wood of these dead branches gets eaten out by termites and consequently there is usually no shortage of nest-holes

In the wild state cockatiels often share their nesting sites with other species; arrows point to nests of a pair of wild cockatiels (left) and ringneck parrots. Photo by Dr. Gerald R. Allen.

Taking in its surroundings while roosting quietly on a perch occupies more time than any other single activity engaged in by cockatiels. Photo by Dr. Gerald R. Allen.

This cockatiel is guarding its nest-log and is engaging in the threat display used by cockatiels to warn off intruders. Photo by Dr. Gerald R. Allen.

Here a cockatiel shows a typical attitude adopted by birds of the family Cacatuidae by thrusting its wings forward; this posture is most often assumed after a flight. Photo by Dr. Gerald R. Allen.

for cockatiels. Fighting for suitable nest sites is also minimal because the cockatiel is not very selective in picking a nesting chamber. The higher holes may be preferred to ones lower down, but any position will do in a pinch and the size of the entrance and the diameter of the inside cavity are practically immaterial. The cockatiel has, after all, no time to be discriminatory, and other factors must bow to this urgency. Depending on the availability of holes, several pairs of cockatiels may nest in the same tree although it is more usual for each pair to select different trees. As the trees are scattered, a breeding flock can thus spread over a large area. Nevertheless, the different pairs will continue to feed and travel to and from the feeding and watering places as a flock.

The pair-bond is not reinforced by the male bird feeding his hen. She has to get her food for herself throughout the nesting period. Consequently the cock bird has to take his turn in incubation and brooding. The independence of the hen toward the male might benefit the species because the pairs may have to range some distance to glean enough food for the chicks, and each parent, through the agency of the flock, will get to know the extent and areas of feeding and just where water is to be found.

When not breeding, the cockatiel is a very sociable bird both with its own kind and toward other birds. It is therefore found in tight little flocks, usually of up to about twenty individuals. However, when a particularly rich supply of food is available, such as freshly harvested fields littered with scattered seeds, or when a long drought has forced them to congregate near the few remaining sources of water, they will form flocks that may consist of hundreds and sometimes thousands. The members of small flocks tend to remain in close company with each other, but the larger groups are noticed to easily break up into smaller units. As they fly, and they move very fast across the sky, it appears that the conspicuous white shoulder flashes and the shrill sounding and often repeated *weel, weel* call serve to keep the members of the flock in close contact with each other. They are so gregarious that when the small flock settle on a dead tree, most birds perch together on the same branch. Yet, despite this

74

Normally living in small flocks in the wild, the cockatiel is basically a social bird, and individuals generally get along well with each other in captivity (at least out of the mating periods). In this regard they are much superior to some other bird species as pets. Photo by Louise van Der Meid.

This is a view taken along the Murchison River in Australia. Cockatiels have been observed to breed at this spot, but not during comparatively dry weather. Photo by Dr. Gerald R. Allen.

Opposite:
This male cockatiel is about eight months old. Photo by Dr. Gerald R. Allen.

liking for company, they do not actually touch one another. Even the mated birds never clump together, as do so many parrots, and should they happen to touch, the birds usually show that they are disturbed by this by raising their crests in mild alarm and by quickly moving a short step or two away and then, contented and relaxed, sit with lowered crests and slightly fluffed feathers for this is the attitude of composure and well-being.

Because they so very noticeably avoid perching on leafy branches and very much prefer to select dead trees, they sometimes have to sit rather closer together than usual on the single branch that is sometimes found near the top of a live tree. This close perching usually causes them to squabble and fight and they will not settle for long. When alighting after a flight, whether to feed on the ground or to settle on a branch, the flock behaves almost as one individual. In the trees they are said to be tame and confiding and can be viewed from a few yards distance without giving them alarm. On the ground it is a different matter, for they are extremely timid and fly upward at the slightest disturbance. As they come in to drink at a waterhole in the early morning and again in the evening they always seem especially afraid and may circle for quite some time before they dare land. When they do land, they usually plummet down to settle in the shallows, rather than landing on the banks and then walking down. They drink with the beak immersed; after a few such hasty gulps the whole flock is off and away from what they seem to treat as a very dangerous place. As almost all desert-loving birds drink if they have the opportunity to do so, avian predators find that watering places are good places to capture the unwary.

It must be of benefit for a migrating or nomadic species of seed-eating bird to live in flocks rather than as isolated pairs or individuals. It is possible for a flock to more quickly search the ground for the richest pickings. If a hawk or another predator decides to attack, it is far more likely to be noticed by one member of the flock, who would give general alarm, before it got too dangerously close. Then, should a predator attack, it would be difficult for it to concentrate

This male outdoor aviary bird is eating seed which has fallen to the ground; in an outdoor aviary, the cockatiels will often spend as much time feeding from the ground as they spend feeding from the feeder. Photo by Dr. Gerald R. Allen.

Individual cockatiels vary as to how many and what kind of baths they will take. Some will jump into and happily splash around in water more than once a day, whereas others will never enter water. Photo by Dr. Gerald R. Allen.

Cockatiels like to chew, especially on natural branches and twigs, and have such items provided. Photo by Dr. Gerald R. Allen.

It is entirely natural behavior for cockatiels to feed by browsing along the ground; in the wild, most of their food is obtained by ground-foraging. Photo by Dr. Gerald R. Allen.

These eggs, carpeted by leaves and grass, were laid in a nest-log in an outdoor aviary; five is the most frequently encountered number of eggs in a cockatiel clutch. Photo by Dr. Gerald R. Allen.

The feet of parrots and a few other birds (including woodpeckers) are known as *zygodactyl*—having two toes pointed forward and two pointed backward. Such feet are well adapted to grasping objects to be eaten or climbed on. Photo by Dr. Gerald R. Allen.

upon a particular bird, as they are all alike, all have a similar movement, and all are jumbled up in the same crowd. Indeed, the cockatiel most likely to be captured would be an injured or sick bird or one that noticeably differed in its color pattern from the others.

Cockatiels, as they walk over the ground searching for food, keep fairly close together, presumably indicating that they do concentrate on the richest patches of food. Such a group of feeding birds will call down other flocks of passing cockatiels by giving their *weel* flocking call. Feeding is very rapid. Each tiny seed is picked up in the bill and rapidly hulled by rotating it with the tongue while the foremost edge of the lower beak works against the inside of the hook of the upper bill. The feet are not used to scrape vegetation or even to steady food. Therefore cockatiels are practically dependent upon ripe seed lying on the ground.

It is interesting that Australia, with perhaps 54 species of parrots, is especially rich in those which take the larger amount of their food from low herbage or the ground. Indeed, no less than 38 species are adapted to this. Although the cockatiel has been reported as sometimes taking berries or the nectar of flowers from trees, it is normally one of the extreme ground-feeding forms. It is said to live largely on the seeds of herbaceous plants and grasses and particularly of the Mitchell grasses, *Astrebla* species. The cockatiel may well be so highly specialized to search and take its seeds as it walks along that, when it is forced to feed on partly hidden seed held in the plant or seed partly covered by dead or live foliage, it is at a disadvantage compared to the partly ground-feeding parrots, the residential species. These residential species of parrot are found where the pasture is of the more permanent kind in association with large or well-foliaged trees, and these, unlike the cockatiel, do turn over vegetation, climb and hold food in the foot to steady it.

Quite irrespective of their sex, all cockatiels will preen one another, but this is more frequently seen in mated pairs. When a cockatiel preens itself on the wings, back, or tail, it does so with its head held high. This head position generally makes other cockatiels keep their distance. But when it

The orange-yellow coloration of the neck and facial region doesn't usually appear on male cockatiels until they have undergone their first moult, which generally occurs when they are about six months old. Photo by Dr. Gerald R. Allen.

Opposite:
Underside view of an adult female cockatiel of the wild-type coloration, showing the pattern of markings on the underside of the tail feathers; these markings are absent in adult males. The finger points to the pelvic region of the bird; experienced breeders can determine sex by checking the relative openness or closeness of the bones in this region. Photo by Manolo Guevara.

While preening itself, a cockatiel will take oil from a gland situated at the base of its tail to use in grooming feathers on other parts of the body. Photo by Dr. Gerald R. Allen.

86

Examples of mutual preening: the birds take turns grooming each
other. Photos by Dr. Gerald R. Allen.

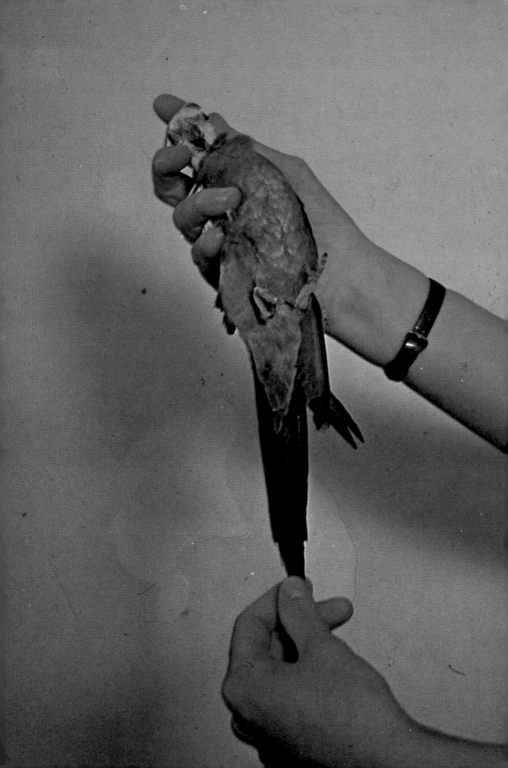

A male cockatiel feeding one of his offspring. The youngster is here perched above its parent, which makes feeding difficult; the more normal position would be with the parent bird on the same level as the baby or slightly above it. Photo by Dr. Gerald R. Allen.

Opposite:
Underside of an adult male cockatiel of the normal (wild-type) coloration; note the absence of a pattern of color on the tail feathers. Photo by Manolo Guevara.

grooms its throat, chest or abdomen its head is held low (a submissive posture), which often causes an adjacent cockatiel to sidle over and attempt to get itself preened by the grooming bird. It does this in a subtle way by adopting a very meek approach. The crest is held tight to the scalp indicating that it means no aggression, the eyes are partially closed, and its head is held very low. In this fawning attitude it will nudge the preening bird gently with its closed bill. Should this not get immediate attention it will repeat the nudging again and again until it does. Eventually the preening bird will pause in its grooming and look around to see who it is that interrupts it; then it is confronted by this most abject-looking cockatiel. To give a vicious peck or take offense at such a contrite-looking bird as the interruptor is simply not done in cockatiel circles. The peck of annoyance is disarmed at once into a preen and once it starts to preen the other it usually will continue to do so for several minutes. The bird being preened slowly moves its head to direct the preening bird's bill into fresh areas. If the grooming stops then it will renudge and start it off once again. Should the other cockatiel not want to oblige, it usually flies off for some peace and quiet. Cockatiels that are very keen to be preened do not necessarily wait for another to begin to preen but solicit such a favor from resting birds, that is ones who look drowsy with their heads held down on their shoulders. The method of approach is the same meekly subservient one.

Males when not partnered are rather fidgety beings and any movement from another cockatiel would catch their eye. It is, therefore, very likely that they would notice any preening bird and fly to its side to beg a preen for themselves. This may well be the manner in which members of a pair become introduced to one another. If the preening bird be another male or an already mated hen; then the bird in search of a partner would be signaled off by the other bird raising its crest or by threatening to peck it and, very seldom, by fighting. Fights between cockatiels are rare.

The Care and Maintenance of Cockatiels

FEEDING

The basic food for captive cockatiels will be seed. It is normal for this to be given as a mixture rather than allow the birds to make their own choice by feeding the several seeds in separate containers. Most often the mix will contain various millets, canary seed and sunflower seed and sometimes wheat, oats, safflower and, in Europe, hemp seed. It will be seen that each bird has its own taste. Some prefer sunflower and others canary seed. There are those that like large amounts of millet, one of the cheapest and least nutritious of seeds, and others that ignore it completely. When a mixture is fed some of the seed may be wasted, unless, that is, it is left until even the least-liked seeds are eaten. The type of seed preferred will sometimes differ. For example, it is commonly found that when the parents are rearing chicks they may decide to eat some particular seed which may have been one for which they have seldom before had any real liking.

The advantage of feeding a seed mix is that it does get the birds to be aware of more seeds and, perhaps, to sample each sort. As each seed type differs in its dietary essentials, what one lacks another may provide.

To someone with a knowledge of mammal and poultry nutrition, it is somewhat surprising that so many species of captive birds are able to live, molt and breed when the single source of nourishment is "bird-seed" and water. This is because the seeds that are commonly fed are grossly deficient in several essentials. Most are, for example, low in total protein; but worse, the protein they do contain is very low in the amino acid lysine. Lysine has importance because the protein of the bird's body has a high percentage of this. Seeds are also deficient in certain vitamins including A, D, B-two

Above and left:
Views of a cockatiel preening itself, showing the great maneuverability of the bird's head while preening the back (left, upper photos) and breast (right, upper photos).
Left:
 In grooming the head feathers, the cockatiel has to use its feet. Photos by Dr. Gerald R. Allen.

Indoors or outdoors, the cockatiel is a lovely bird, but its sedate beauty can best be appreciated in a natural outdoor setting. Photo by Dr. Gerald R. Allen.

This baby cockatiel was raised in a nest-log in an outdoor aviary in Australia. Here it has just emerged from the log and is inspecting its surroundings before attempting to fly for the first time. Photo by Dr. Gerald R. Allen.

(riboflavin), and B-twelve (cyanocobalamin) and are low in many minerals including sodium salts, an important substance in animal tissues, and calcium. Calcium is an essential part of bone tissue and of egg shells.

Millet seed contains only about 12% protein, and canary seed about 18%, which is, incidentally, of a higher quality. Sunflower seed is primarily grown as an oil seed, consequently the plant breeders have concentrated on raising this to a maximum and the protein and carbohydrate levels are

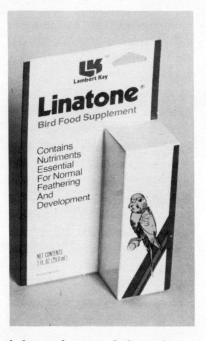

Vitamin and mineral supplements that can be used to fortify the basic cockatiel diet in captivity are economical and easy to use.

much less substantial than they were in the past. Cockatiels live on a diet of seeds for years and years and may even breed; but it is not possible to raise good quality youngsters on these alone, largely because of the lack of lysine. As we shall see in the chapter on aviary breeding, the simplest way of providing supplementary lysine is to give the birds cow's milk, either as bread sop or in the drinking water. Cuttlefish bone will provide many of the minerals, and if green food can be given this will satisfy the requirements for trace minerals.

Like other seed-eating captive birds, it is obvious that the cockatiel has been highly specialized by natural selection to make the most of a largely cereal grain diet. Some of the vitamin deficiencies of the seed are overcome by eating small quantities of old and fresh feces. Bacterial activity in the bowel of the bird and after being voided produce many vitamins of the B series, including B-two and B-twelve. Although eating feces may seem particularly perverse, it is a common practice of many animals, including rabbits, which pass two types of pellet: the hard sort known to all pet keepers and a softer pellet that is eaten directly from the anus. Dogs, and especially puppies, require more vitamin B than the diet can give, and they take to eating the droppings of herbivores such as horses and, in the absence of these, the feces of dogs, including their own. In birds, turkey-buzzards in South America are said to eat the feces of any mammal the second they are voided. This practice has been studied in the budgerigar, where it seems that unless they are allowed to eat some of their own stool they begin to suffer anemia from lack of vitamin B-twelve. Eating feces to re-digest food and so obtain extra benefit is called *refection*. Refection has to be distinguished from *coprophagy*, which is a pathological or psychological condition in which feces are eaten by an individual of a species in which this is otherwise unknown.

Cockatiels can also manage on such a poor fare by being so supremely efficient in their digestive mechanism that they can remove practically every molecule of the scarce necessities from the grain. Most animals and birds could only achieve this by eating such large masses of this imbalanced food that by its very bulk they would get sufficient necessities. The best example to be given of this would be the Irish people who, before the terrible potato famines of the nineteenth century, depended largely on the "Irish" potato, which is very low in total protein. Consequently their appetite for this vegetable was gargantuan, and the Irishman was said to have to eat a stone (14 lbs.) a day to escape suffering from a protein deficiency. But cockatiels live on a poor diet by managing through their metabolism to be supremely conservative in the body's turnover of these substances.

Young cockatiels are gregarious and usually perch in the vicinity of their parents and siblings. Photo by Dr. Gerald R. Allen.

This photo shows the actual first venture into flight of a baby cockatiel. The birds are relatively clumsy at first but soon gain proficiency. Photo by Dr. Gerald R. Allen.

The sunshine of the day produces vitamin D from the oils on the exposed skin of the body. Calcium, needed for egg laying, is stored well beforehand in the bones of the limbs. There should be a lesser need for the bird to scrimp and save from its meager food if this is supplemented as suggested. Through the year the author's entire parrot collection has had added to their drinking water a proprietary water-soluble mixture of vitamins and trace elements sold for use in the poultry and livestock industry.

BREEDING ACCOMMODATIONS

The usual way of breeding cockatiels is in small garden aviaries with one pair of birds to each flight. This method stops fighting over nest accomodations and ensures that the breeder's choice of pairings is kept. Certain male cockatiels can be quite promiscuous and if their own mate is indifferent to their attentions they could pay successful court to another's mate.

Breeding pairs of cockatiels in this outdoor garden aviary are partitioned off from their neighboring pairs by wire screening, but the birds can see each other. They are often stimulated into breeding by observing the actions of nearby breeding pairs. Photo by Brian Seed.

Cockatiels are so gregarious that whole blocks of adjacent aviaries can be constructed with a considerable benefit to breeding success, as once some pairs start to breed others will be stimulated by their example. This is precisely as with the budgerigar, which as is well-known can be difficult to breed if only a single pair is kept. The block method of construction for aviaries is the most economical way of building flights, as other than the two ends the sides of each aviary are shared and a single entrance door will do for a whole range of shelters. Double wiring between adjacent aviaries is very necessary with most parrots to prevent them injuring each other and their recently fledged chicks by fighting and clinging to the separate wire. Double-wiring is

Seeds are the staple fixtures of the cockatiel's diet and can be purchased either by individual type of seed or in the form of seed mixtures. Owners of just one or a few birds usually purchase the excellent seed mixes available at pet shops instead of buying individual seeds by bulk and formulating their own mixtures. Photo by Brian Seed.

not usually essential for cockatiels. They seldom fall out with each other unless the mistake has been made of fastening the nest-box of one pen too near that in the adjacent flight.

A large aviary can hold more than one pair of breeding cockatiels. However if the flight is not greater than, say, ten feet in length they are best restricted to only one pair although other species of birds can be kept, including doves, canaries, or foreign finches. If quail and pheasants are to be kept the lid of the cockatiel's nest-box should be wired off to prevent these heavy birds from roosting on its lid.

Feed supplements designed to give a bird the capacity to meet the extra demands made on its metabolism at breeding time can be valuable if wisely used, but of course the best system to use is to make sure that your cockatiels are always well-enough looked after that they don't require special breeding conditioners.

The height of an aviary should always be higher than the height of the owner and, to avoid unnecessary cutting of the wire, as wide as a roll of wire netting, which is usually three feet. The total length of the flight need not exceed six feet. From the point of view of the cockatiel it would be better if it were as long as possible. If other birds are kept, it is a good principle to build the aviaries as large as the available land and finances permit. They can always be subdivided if this later proves necessary.

To the back of each flight is attached a small well-lit shelter in which the bird can be locked to roost in bad weather. It will be found that most cockatiels do in fact prefer to sleep in such a shelter. The shelter also gives a dry place for the seed. It will be found that if the floor of the shelter is at table height and has a common feeding passage with the other row of aviaries behind this, feeding and cleaning are

Perches of different diameters allow the birds to vary their grip and therefore not have to hold their feet in the same position all the time, and the use of natural twigs and branches lets the birds have something to nibble on. Photo by Brian Seed.

easy. The high floor of the shelter also makes the seed less accessible to mice. As cockatiels do not like having to descend to natural floor level inside the confines of a shelter to feed, the birds are more relaxed. Next to the seed dishes should be the drinking water. A further water supply, held in a shallow bowl, might well be placed in the flight to serve as a bath. Cockatiels soak themselves in water when breeding to humidify the nest-box. Likewise green food and other tid bits can be put with the seed and water in the shelter. It might be more convenient if a further small feeding platform could be attached to the front wire of the flight so that it can be filled from a small outside door. When the sun has little strength to it, the daily portion of bread dipped in milk can also be placed on this platform. Usually the bread and milk rearing food would be fed in a saucer inside the shelter.

Natural branches make the best perches, for the birds can busy themselves chewing the bark. The differing diameters of the twigs exercise the birds' toes in a way that standard width dowel perching cannot do. It is surprising how a seemingly well-fixed perch can sometimes work loose simply from the weight of the bird taking off and landing. Perches ought, therefore, to be firmly fixed by either wiring or nailing them in position rather than wedging them in place. However, this does not mean that perches must be rigid and unyielding; so long as one end is secure the other can be left free to give a natural spring. Some horizontal perches have to be rigid enough to let the birds hold their position when pairing. Too great an amount of twigs and foliage in a flight may so frighten the cockatiel that they may barely dare to leave the safety of the shelter. The perches are placed to give a maximum of flying room. To do this the two are fastened about a foot down from the roof and a foot from either end of the flight. Between the two high perches should be affixed another perch low enough to the ground that someone entering the flight can easily step over it. The low central perch is used as much as, if not more than, the higher ones.

It is not always mentioned, but cockatiels can sometimes breed most successfully in cages. Against this practice it is said that when parent parrots cannot be allowed to fly freely, as in an aviary, then any youngsters they hatch will be deformed or disabled in some way. *This is nonsense!* The health and well-being of any chick depends entirely upon its nutrition and its hereditary make-up. Therefore, exactly as with aviary birds, provided that the parents are not closely related and carry no lethal or semi-lethal genes and their feeding is good, the chicks born to caged parents will be every bit as good in their rearing as they would in an aviary. This does not say that it is not better to have aviary accommodation, for what aviaries do give is a better chance of the parents' being able to fulfill a more normal breeding behavior pattern.

A nest box attached to a cage; the back of the nest box has been left off to show the removable egg-board and its scooped indentation. Photo by Miceli Studios.

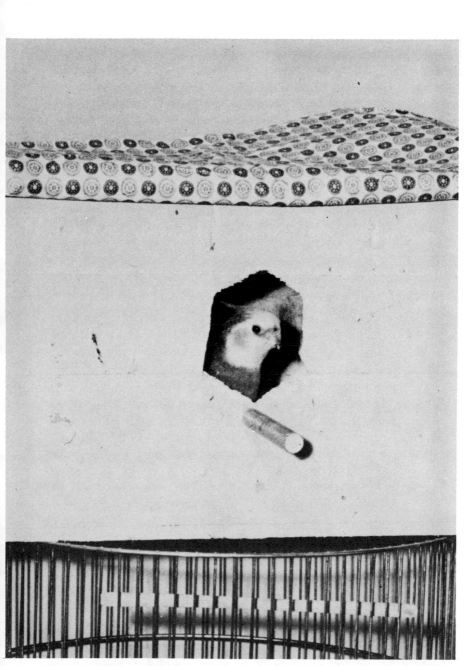

This cockatiel nest-box sits atop a cylindrical cage and provides secure quarters for the breeding pair; the male is visible at the entrance hole. Photo by Dr. Herbert R. Axelrod.

For example, part of normal male courtship consists of flying to and fro in the near vicinity of the nest. It might therefore help the fertility of a caged pair, although not necessarily so, if the cock bird were able to fly from one perch to another, rather than—as they almost always do in a cage—scrambling along the wire. Likewise it might be that, in some circumstances, a small cage may be at a disadvantage because in the natural state of things the non-incubating parent sits some little distance away from the nesting chamber. If forced to sit too near, as it has to in a cage, and because it cannot otherwise be engaged in some activity or other, it may be enticed to enter the nest more frequently than is usual. This could disrupt the pattern of incubation between the sexes. But these are all hypotheses. Cage-bred budgerigars are in every way just as good as those bred in larger surroundings.

It will give more area to the caged cockatiel when their nest-box is hung outside the cage. In any case the cage must always be as large as possible. Those people known to the author who have been successful in cage-breeding cockatiels have let the parents fly loose in the room on occasion. It is absolutely essential that only one pair of breeding cockatiels be confined to each cage, otherwise there is a chance that murder will be done should they squabble, because the defeated bird will be unable to escape from its persecutor.

GENERAL POINTS

Although cockatiels may come from desert regions, they cannot withstand the full force of the sun upon their heads for days on end. Cages therefore ought not to be placed in full sunlight unless a patch of shade falls on the cage. If a parrot is housed for long periods with little to occupy its time, it will inevitably get bored. To give itself something to do the parrot may well start eating when it is not really hungry and so become fat. It may over-preen and from this begin to pluck feathers from itself. Others may scream incessantly or pace ceaselessly from one end of the cage to the other; most just sit out their time. But this is wrong. They are active birds in nature, and to become a feathered vegetable

This cage is situated in a corner so that it does not receive continuous full daylight but still gets some occasional natural light. Photo by Dr. Herbert R. Axelrod.

Cockatiels are inquisitive and playful and should be provided with toys to help keep them amused. Photo by Dr. Herbert R. Axelrod.

instead of a bird cannot be right. Something to occupy its attention is needed. Toys such as ping-pong balls or blocks of wood and, especially, a mirror are most useful. One, at least, of the perches ought to be taken out and a natural branchlet cut to replace it. The perches provided with cages are of some hard, unchewable wood and are mere furniture. But a natural, stout twig can be pared at and eventually turned into splinters over several days or weeks of enjoyment.

Two birds in the same cage are not the answer for boredom. They may entertain one another to some degree, but boredom again sets in, and what better to do but preen the other's head? This turns almost all caged pairs of cockatiels into little bare-headed vultures. The ear patch and the crest are particularly attacked. Once the crest is lost the bird cannot signal discontent or anger to its partner, and this aggravates the mutilation even further. If two birds must share the same cage, the best way of overcoming boredom and mutilation is to let them have the opportunity to breed.

Breeding Cockatiels

Generally cockatiels are extremely easy to breed. If they are satisfied with the nesting arrangements some hens will lay and may even incubate though they have no mates. However, such unmated hens most probably would have laid days, weeks or even years earlier had they been courted by a male. For one of the purposes of courtship is to stimulate the reproductive processes of the hen. Male cockatiels will court throughout the year, and it is possible for some hens to breed the year around. Yet better fortune seems to attend those clutches that are laid in the spring and summer. This is partly because cockatiels are affected by both weather and the time of the year. During short days they are not quite so keen to breed and, if they do, they frequently have a high level of infertility. They also have less daylight in which to feed their chicks. Then, too, adult cockatiels begin to molt in the early autumn, just as do the early-hatched chicks of the current year. Frequently parents in molt become very lackadaisical about caring for the chicks they have or about incubating their eggs. Cold weather not infrequently fatally chills both eggs and chicks. Yet in warmer climates such as South Africa, Florida and California, some of these adverse factors cannot apply and breeding results in the shorter days of the year are often quite as good, if not better, than in their summers when the days can be too hot.

Nevertheless, in temperate climates, and particularly in Britain and the eastern and central states of the U.S.A., it is better to take down all the nest-boxes in the autumn, putting them back in the spring when it is noticed that the wild birds are beginning to nest. This will usually be by the middle of March. During a breeding season of this length two or three clutches should be raised, so that a fertile pair ought to be able to produce at least six youngsters. Twice this number could be reared by well-tried pairs.

SEXUAL MATURITY

The white and black cockatoos are generally held to take two or three years to reach sexual maturity; however, the smaller-sized cockatiel is rather precocious, as most will breed and prove fully fertile at six months of age. Several pairs known to the author have laid fertile clutches when the parents were exactly four months old. However, at these ages the parents often prove incompetent and their precocity comes to nothing. Once they do achieve sexual maturity, they seem to keep their fertility for many years. Perfectly good youngsters can be obtained from parents that are in their early twenties.

If several different pairs are to be kept for breeding, it is good policy to arrange that an experienced bird gets paired with an innocent one. This, in practice, generally means that each youngster gets an older mate. Reproduction comes perfectly naturally to cockatiels and their success as parents improves with age. Indeed, old birds that have never been given the chance to breed almost always prove to be ideal parents; this could never be said of the young. Experience may also be important as it is not infrequent that birds found to be hopeless as parents one year can become model parents the next.

Cockatiels have particularly strong pair-bonds or marriage ties. It is generally accepted, again with no real evidence, that in the wild a pair may remain together until death separates them. Therefore, when pairing them up, try to do so several months before it is intended they should be allowed to breed to give them plenty of time to become fully acquainted with each other. Birds that are complete strangers to one another will form an almost immediate union, but if one has been previously mated to another and can still hear or see the previous mate when re-paired, they may refuse to have anything to do with the second bird. As with budgerigars, it might be better when the birds are not breeding to house the males together in one set of flights and the

This young female cockatiel is fully mature sexually. Cockatiels generally are able to breed by the time they are about half a year old, but their first breeding attempts are not always successful. Photo by Harry V. Lacey.

females in another, the two groups separated by as much distance as possible. In this case they cannot form ties with each other and they need only a month together before being provided with nest-boxes since they will form an almost immediate bond.

The semen is extremely long-lived so it may take a month or more before a hen becomes unable to lay fertile eggs after she was last mated. Therefore the offspring of a paired hen cannot be definitely said to be the children of her present mate if the eggs were laid within a month of her being taken away from a previous partner. This is a further reason, if one wishes to breed "pedigree" cockatiels, why pairs should be put together for some weeks before they are allowed to lay.

Lastly, anyone setting out to breed birds ought to accept at the outset that a completely successful breeding year has never yet come for anyone, nor is likely to do so. Disappointments are inevitable. The only really satisfactory way of remaining permanently cheerful is to directly adopt the most pessimistic of attitudes as to the eventual outcome. Take it that most pairs will not lay, the eggs will be infertile, that pairs will not sit, that chicks will die along with the parents, etc. And when none of these disasters happen, then that is a reason for being happy; and when they do—well, they were expected after all. Joking to one side, several disappointments can be overcome if many pairs can be synchronized. Then pairs with low fertility can have their bad eggs exchanged for a clutch of good ones from another pair. Or their single chick can be slowly built up to a full clutch by robbing a more fertile pair of their chicks at the rate of one a day. Too often people who foster would do the reverse, putting the smaller clutch in with the bigger and so allow the less fertile pair a second chance. If cockatiels are robbed of their chicks or eggs they usually lay again within a week and no harm will follow.

NEST-BOXES

One can often read of cockatiels laying behind a brick or in a dark corner of their shelter because their nest-box was unsuitable or because they were not provided with one. But most pairs refuse to nest unless they have a nest-box. In the wild they use holes in trees, the eggs being laid on the bare wood with no attempt at making a nest of any kind. But for the aviculturalist logs with suitable holes already bored in them are far from easy to come by. If they can be gotten, the log is usually almost too heavy to handle and the holes tend to be any size but the diameter that is wanted. The cumbersome shape and roundness of the log make them particularly difficult to hang. Logs cannot even be thought of as a perfect way of escaping the carpentry of building a box, for they really require an inspection door and, as the hole often goes right through, a bottom and a top have to be made and fastened on. To upset things further, many natural holes have been previously used by wild birds, and fleas from these previous tenants can become a severe pest in warm weather. After much experimenting with natural cavities and comparing breeding success with wooden boxes, there can be no doubt that a well-constructed wooden box is infinitely superior to the natural product for aviary breeding.

Except when breeding is restricted to the warmer months of the year, it is advised that nest-boxes be well made with tight joints and quite thick walls and bottom so that they will retain the maximum of heat. Planks of natural wood, although superb in some ways, are very heavy to manipulate, expensive to buy and will warp and alter their size with the humidity of the air. It is always advisable when building a nest-box, and the more so when using planks of natural wood, to use screws rather than nails to reduce movement of the wood and opening up joints. Screws have considerable advantage when rebuilding or repair of a nest-box has to take place. If larger parrots than cockatiels are kept then screws become essential, for their boxes will have to be entirely taken apart and rebuilt annually to ensure continual success in their breeding.

The very best of all material for nest-boxes is heavy exterior-grade plywood. As this is widely used to retain poured concrete, it can sometimes be acquired very cheaply second-hand from building sites. Even if heavy-ply may sometimes "sweat" with condensation in the winter, this will not prove any inconvenience to the birds. Its advantage over other materials is that it withstands most parrots' chewing and, when machine cut, makes perfect joints because it is not affected by the weather. Interior-grade plywood can only be of temporary service as it generally begins to peel apart within a year, yet even so it is warm and costs far less than resin-bonded plywood. Chipboard is a material that is never recommended for any outdoor work and yet proves to be far more durable than might be imagined. It is particularly warm, compares in cheapness with interior plywood, and when it is covered with a layer of non-toxic paint or varnish, its life is increased by years. The main fault, apart from its lack of strength to resist intensive chewing by the parrots, is that the screws or nails that hold the box together direct water into the chipboard and cause it to "corrode" at these sites. This makes rebuilding or modification of chipboard-built boxes very difficult indeed.

In this roughly constructed home-made nesting box the entrance hole and perch are near the top of the box, set off center to create irregular illumination of the interior. Photo by Brian Seed.

The interior of the nesting-box should be roomy enough to house both parents and developing young without crowding them too much, yet not big enough to cause squabbling between the parents about where the eggs should be incubated. Photo by Dr. Herbert R. Axelrod.

The hole for the cockatiels to enter the nest-box need not be larger that 2½ inches in diameter. If larger than this the entry of rain or light can make it less comfortable for the birds and if the entrance is less than two inches across the cockatiels cannot crawl through it. Traditionally the entrance hole is circular. It is far more simple to make a square entrance by cutting off one of the top corners with two saw cuts before finally assembling the box. It is also usual for the hole to lie at the center of the front, but if the hole is made to one side this gives a less evenly illuminated inside to the box and the parent birds have some choice as to the amount of light they wish to have on their nest. A square hole in a corner weakens the face side of the box far less than a central hole which, in any case, must always be made lower down the face of the box and the amount of room above the entrance hole is so much wasted wood. Directly under the entrance hole a perch should be fastened so that a cockatiel standing upon this may look directly into the entrance hole.

The male cockatiel avidly inspects both the nest hollow itself and the vicinity immediately surrounding the nest before signalling the female that he has found a suitable spot. Photo by Dr. Gerald R. Allen.

This breeding pair has given its nest-log breeding site approval after a thorough inspection; inspection of the breeding site is a very important phase of the courtship/breeding process. Photo by Dr. Gerald R. Allen.

There is really no need for the height of the box to be greater than eighteen inches. Even this generous height can result in the parents dropping down rather hastily onto the chicks and possibly fatally rupturing a chick's liver. The usual size for a cockatiel's nest-box is about a foot high at the back and an inch taller at the front. The difference in height gives the slope to the roof which falls away from the entrance hole. The roof might well be made to overlap the sides and back by a half inch to prevent water running back inside the box.

Wild parrots frequently are reported as nesting in extremely small cavities. Yet if we imagine six well-grown cockatiel chicks together with their parents they would seem to need a floor area of not less than six inches square. If the inside measurement of the box is larger than an eight-inch square the amount of room given is unnecessarily large for small chicks. If the floor area is extensive the parents may well differ as to where the exact site for incubation is to take place and the eggs can get rolled about and broken. The ideal inside measurement for the box might be eight inches square, yet screwed to the sides of this base are four lengths of 1½-inch-square sticks. The sticks give an over-all inside measurement of five inches square. This construction means that as the chicks grow they are moved upward day by day by the litter that accumulates, and by the time that they begin to feather they are occupying the maximum eight-inch floor area and are sitting on the sticks.

To descend, the cockatiels need a ladder of wire netting with all loose pieces removed and fastened from the inside of the entrance hole almost down to the bottom of the box.

There may well be those who prefer to leave their breeding pairs of cockatiels alone, and yet even these cautious members of the "leave-it-alone-and-it-will-get-better" school will sometimes have to look inside their boxes. Perhaps this will be to only add some fresh sawdust or to remove an infertile clutch of eggs and, not unlikely, should they notice blow flies hanging around the entrance hole attracted by a dead chick. It will be found that cockatiels tend to panic when they are looked at from above. They scuttle about the base of the nest-box and may smash the eggs by knocking them together or scatter and injure the chicks. The parents cannot very well move away out of the entrance hole as they would have to move upward toward the person frightening them.

The lid of the box therefore makes a poor examination door. Some time or other it could be blown open by the wind and cause the birds to desert or let the rain in. Nor can it give such a good waterproof cover as it would were it screwed down tightly. The better place for the examination door is to one side or to the back of the box. This door is cut about six inches from the bottom to reduce drafts and prevent eggs or chicks from accidentally falling out. It is found that when this type of examination door at the side is opened up, the parent cockatiels usually remain sitting. If they do, it is easy to slip a hand under the bird to feel the eggs or examine the chicks. The parent birds may rock and hiss and sometimes pretend to bite, but it is quite safe to do this. Certain of the more nervous birds will, as the examination door is opened, move out of the box by the entrance hole, but this mild fright will not cause them to desert. A few minutes after they leave either they are back inside or their partner is.

In general cockatiels become alarmed by overhanging vegetation. The best place for a nest-box is, therefore, not in the shelter but in the flight. It is noticeable with aviary birds that although very tame when the owner is outside, they panic with fear if the aviary is entered. And fear, being contagious, spreads right along the row of aviaries causing all the more nervous birds to leave their nests and chicks to squawk and rock from side to side. The place to fasten the boxes is where the contents can be examined without having to enter the aviary at all. This is done by simply fastening the box to the outside of the flight. The cockatiels enter by crawling through a hole cut in the wire where this passes flush over the entrance hole. Another variation of the same idea is to have a short horizontal shelf running along the inside of the wire netting. When the box is unscrewed and removed in the autumn the wire door that covers the hole in the netting is replaced until the next breeding season begins.

A young cockatiel peering out of the entrance hole to its nest-box. In this box the entrance hole is situated about at the center of the upper third of the box; the perch extends through the wall of the box and can be perched on from either inside or outside. Photo by Louise van Der Meid.

The boxes should be looked into each day as the person attending the birds walks along the front of the aviaries topping up the water and changing and seeing to the food. Such a regularity of examination gets the birds quite familiar with the process of opening and closing doors, and they come to accept it as being a normal part of their breeding lives. It ought to be strongly re-emphasized that every nest-box must be screwed or so fastened in position that it cannot be rocked by the wind or accidentally dislodged in some way.

THE EGGS

The eggs are usually laid directly onto the floor of the box with no attempt at making a nest except, perhaps, by chewing a few splinters from the wood to make a thin litter on the floor. It will save eggs getting smashed through rolling if the bottom of the box is made slightly concave to receive the eggs. (A concave base is a standard item in commercially-made budgerigar nest-boxes). Before the nest-box is hung up a small handful of coarse sawdust is put inside to absorb the feces of the chicks. This also helps prevent the eggs from getting cracked by knocking against each other. Many breeders add several inches of damp peat as a "filler" for all their parrot nest-boxes. This is rammed home tight and gives a nice, yielding surface. Against this well-established practice is the knowledge that peat, when it loses its moisture, becomes very dusty and might affect the eyes and the lungs of the young birds. Before it does dry it must make an uncomfortable bed upon which to incubate. It is said that such a damp filling is essential for success, and yet no proof is offered that this is so. Experiments show that a permanent dampness in the box does not increase the hatchability of cockatiel eggs; indeed usually the reverse is true. Parent cockatiels in dry weather often return to their incubation absolutely dripping with moisture from having soaked themselves in their bathing water, and this is all the moisture that cockatiel eggs need.

As the chicks grow, should the box look a little soiled a small quantity of coarse, clean sawdust can be sprinkled inside. However, never add more than a little at a time as too

These cockatiel eggs were laid in soft woody material that lined the bottom of the nest-box. Any filler material used to line the bottom of the nest-box should be free from excess moisture. Photo by Brian Seed.

much will alter both the appearance and the feel of the box and may disturb the parents and cause them to shuffle the chicks about. Young chicks always shuffle themselves backward out from the warm pile (their brothers and sisters) and deposit their feces in a ring an inch or two away from the nest hollow. In a dry climate these droppings soon powder up. But as the chicks grow and begin to move actively about they seem to become less particular as to where they deposit their feces and the whole nest becomes soiled. Yet the nest invariably seems to keep dry, although in a damp climate it may foul up and smell of ammonia. Should the nest-box allow water to leak in and if the weather is cold, then all the chicks can develop a form of arthritis of the feet from the cold and caking "mud," and this deformity persists throughout their lives.

BREEDING

Young males when about three months old or, more precisely, when they have left the nest some four to five weeks, start to give their display call. It may, to some ears, sound like *Cock-ee, cock-ee* or, perhaps, *Joe-ey, Joe-ey* or *Were-it, were-it*. In adult males the song becomes extended by introducing into it various twitterings and warblings. Hens can make none of these calls. As they become adult, males will fly up and down the aviary making this rather high-pitched and sometimes very irritating call with a persistance that seems remarkable. This call is also given when perched and when so doing the wings are pulled away from the body at the shoulders, giving the top of the bird a kite-shaped outline. At this time his crest is lowered, while his head is twisted first one way then the other as he stands facing his hen a little distance away. The hen usually seems undisturbed by his posturing as do other males. Except for the flattened wings and the song, the courting male's posturing is not unlike that of one bird soliciting a preen from another. If the hen is on the ground the male will fussily follow his mate, rather like a courting pigeon. Every now and again he will give a little jump as he warbles, male-calls, and twitters, but he does not seem at ease and his raised crest shows this.

The hen solicits for mating by lowering herself onto the perch with her wings slightly away from the body and flattening her back. She holds her crest down and keeps her head twisted on one side. She does this as the male approaches during one of his courting songs and he, still singing and chortling away, may step directly onto her back. More usually he advances and retreats once or twice, facing first one way and then another, as if uncertain before he does so. The actual pairing takes some little while, and the male may continue singing as he first mounts, but he soon becomes quiet. The female however (Zann believes that it is the male) gives a continual squeaking note. If they have a nest-box it is seen that most mating takes place shortly after the hen comes out of the box. Box or not, mating usually takes place several times a day.

During copulation the male mounts the female from the rear while the female keeps her wings spread; several copulations a day may occur during the breeding period. Photo by Dr. Gerald R. Allen.

Other than cockatiels and some other cockatoos, most male parrots feed the hen during the courtship and nesting period. There is one exception known to the author, and that is a hen cockatiel belonging to Mr. Bill Howarth who pleads to be fed, as do young cockatiels, by bobbing her head and gives a harsh-sounding squeaking call. All the male cockatiels that have been paired to this hen have fed her. This seems to prove that courtship feeding may be done by the male in response to a hen parrot's pleading.

Usually, once a cockatiel's nest-box is hung up the male begins to take a very great interest in it as may his "wife," but to a lesser degree. He will hover about its vicinity and look into the entrance hole and, seemingly, "court" the box by singing and chortling with his wings flattened and his head lowered. It is not usually very long before he gains enough courage to enter, and when inside he will continue singing

In the majority of cases, the male cockatiel will share both pre-incubation and post-incubation care of the eggs and chicks. Photo by Brian Seed.

and may tap with his beak. He often comes and goes into the entrance hole and by his attitude is obviously trying to attract the attention of his "wife" to the box. Not that she is uninterested, but her approach has more caution. So she allows him to do almost all of the preliminary investigation. Soon she too will enter and both of them will spend much of the subsequent days coming and going. Before the hen lays she will spend ever more of her time well within the box chewing the inside wood or brooding at the eventual nest site. The male meantime usually chews around the entrance hole and may, by so doing, enlarge it slightly.

A curious thing to see is how they can enter the box by going in tail first. They most often do this if the lid of the box protrudes sufficiently far over to allow them to lower themselves by their beak while they very neatly slip the tail followed by the body into the entrance hole. No matter how tame a pair of cockatiels are, they are always very cautious about being seen as they come out of the box. If they are alarmed doing this, they ever so slowly slink backwards into the darkness of its cavity.

EGG LAYING

It is wonderfully amazing how soon a hen can begin her clutch once a nest-box is provided. The first egg can be laid in as short a time as three days, although four is usually the earliest time noted. Not that all cockatiels are this quick; the average time for egg laying must be weeks rather than days. Before she lays, the hen usually sleeps outside the nest-box. It is generally found that towards dusk one evening she will slink back inside to spend the night within, and that night is usually the night that she lays her first egg.

The usual size of the clutch will be five eggs. The interval between each successive egg is slightly less than two days. During the laying the hen spends almost all of her time inside the box. The male may be inside with her, but generally he keeps perched nearby. As most males share the incubation and brooding of the young, the number of eggs laid by the hen can fairly accurately be guessed at by noticing how many days it takes the male to begin to incubate inside the

Above: Cockatiel eggs compared to a chicken egg. Photo by Manolo Guevara. *Below:* A cockatiel egg (larger) compared to budgerigar egg. Photo by Miceli Studios.

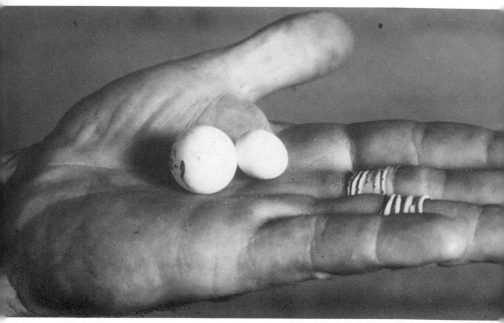

Cockatiel eggs photographed on à $10 bill for size comparison. Photo by Brian Seed.

box, leaving the hen outside, and dividing by two. An occasional hen will take all the incubation duties upon herself, but this is rare because most males will insist on doing their stint. Sometimes both sexes incubate together, and this is especially so toward the end of the incubation when the eggs have started to hatch and the parent birds can, undoubtedly, hear the chicks calling from within their shells. Otherwise the male incubates for most of the daylight hours and the hen overnight, exactly the pattern followed by pigeons and doves.

Inspecting a brood housed in a plywood nest-box equipped with a removable hardboard side partition.

This is a commercially made nest box of the kind sold in pet shops. A nest-box of this type is not intended for outdoor use and therefore needs no slope to its top to allow rain run-off. The hardboard back partition comes in two sections, allowing the lower half to remain in position when the upper half is removed during inspection. Photo by Miceli Studios.

Like the eggs of all parrots, they are white and can be any shape from almost spherical to long and pointed but are usually fat-egg-shaped. They weigh about 6.5 grams, about a thirteenth of the weight of the laying hen cockatiel. Once a hen has laid eggs of a certain shape she usually continues to lay similar eggs. If eggs are to be fostered off under other cockatiels, or if the hen seems to persist in laying well beyond the normal five or six, then the eggs should be marked with an indelible felt-tipped pen. In the case of the persistent layer, if she eventually starts to sit the earlier laid eggs ought to have been fostered elsewhere or destroyed because the whole clutch will be lost through chilling if the parents try to incubate too many.

A cockatiel about to take over the incubation appears to do so without any "exchange ceremony" as do many birds. Instead the one about to take over simply sits down next to the already incubating bird. The two may brood together for a while, each, usually, taking part of the clutch. Far more typically, as one sits down the other gets up and leaves the nest. As one of the few times that adult cockatiels sit physically touching is when they share incubation or brooding, it might well be this natural dislike of close contact that makes the previously brooding bird leave the nest as the other settles down beside it.

INCUBATION AND REARING OF THE CHICKS

The most frequent incubation time for cockatiel eggs is nineteen days. But cold weather or indifferent incubation can lengthen the time of hatching days in excess of this. The chicks hatch in the sequence in which the eggs were laid, at roughly two-day intervals. However, as incubation seldom starts with the first egg, and not always until three or four have been laid, very often the first group hatch almost simultaneously. Strangely for parrots, cockatiels sometimes remove parts of the eggshells, for these can be found in the flight.

On hatching, the chicks are very helpless with such huge heads on such frail bodies that is doubtful if they can raise their heads in the air. The beak is quite soft to the touch and

Two of the chicks from this group of six eggs laid have hatched and have the typically helpless and ugly appearance of baby birds. Photo by Harry V. Lacey.

is tipped for ten days or so with the hard white egg-tooth that it has used to cut its way through the eggshell. The eyes are sealed, and the whole appearance is very embryonic-looking. Long wisps of yellow down clothe the body and top of the head. The intensity of the yellow down varies somewhat, and it has been found that the yellower the chick the yellower the pigmentation of the adult. When the first albino does occur, contrary to all previous cockatiel chicks it will have a pure white down. The dark eyes of the chicks can be seen under the skin of the eyelids, but lutinos have an inherited defect that makes them unable to synthesize black pigments and therefore they have pink eyes under the skin.

A pair of opaline cockatiels. The male (at right) is moulting into normal plumage. Photo by Brian Seed.

At first the chicks have a cheeping call which they give when they are disturbed in some way, and this or a similar noise is made when they are hungry or are being fed. If a very tame cockatiel is watched feeding her babies she will be seen to quite delicately take the bill of a calling chick into her own. The slight pinch she gives it makes the chick bob its head vigorously, and this causes the parent to push regurgitated food into the sides of the chick's beak with her tongue. The chick, while she is doing this, keeps up a continual encouraging cheeping noise. During the exchange of food it will be noticed that while most of the food is obviously crop-softened partly digested seed, some quantity of sticky, slightly milky fluid accompanies it. If the chick is then taken in the hand and examined under a strong light, for the crop wall and the skin are quite translucent, a mass of seed grit and surprisingly little fluid will be seen. Although parent parrots do not have the necessary glandular structure within the crop with which to secrete "crop milk" as do pigeons, it is obvious that some proteinaceous substances must be included with the food they regurgitate because the rapid growth of the chicks could not be maintained on seed alone. In the budgerigar the "true" stomach or proventriculus, which lies between the crop and gizzard, becomes much enlarged during the rearing period. It seems most likely, even if it has to yet be proved experimentally, that some of the proventricular contents, including its glandular secretions, are fed to the chicks. It may be this, as well as spittle and cells from the gullet and crop, which is the source of extra protein for the chick.

On hatching and for a few days afterward, the skin of cockatiel chicks is so translucent that almost all the internal organs can be made out. The most noticeable feature is the gizzard, giving a huge bulge to the belly. The gizzard of birds is a muscular part of the bowel that grinds, perhaps "chews" is the better verb, the crop-and proventriculus-softened food into small particles using as teeth small pieces of gravel and grit, and once parent parrots have chicks they become noticeably much keener to collect this than previously. The second feature to strike notice is the huge size of the crop. It is no exaggeration to say that some cockatiel chicks, with particularly good parents, have a crop that in size almost exceeds that of the body. Sometimes bubbles of air get swallowed by the chicks and can be seen inside the crop. These cannot possibly affect the digestion of the chick, are perfectly natural, and might be ignored. However, if the crop becomes greatly distended with air, enough to cause worry, this can be removed simply by gently squeezing the crop between the fingers and thumb and pushing in a slightly upward direction, when the air will escape through the infant's mouth.

A freshly hatched chick cannot maintain its body temperature. If it is not brooded continuously its temperature will fall; it will become increasingly stupefied. It can withstand this cooling for a time, but eventually it will die. Even if warmed up the cooling may have affected its resistance to disease and later it may die. Should chicks be allowed by the parents to get chilled, it is better to take them away to hand-rear them or foster them off with others.

At about the time that the feathers begin to "pin," the babies first acquire an ability to control their body temperature. But as pin feathers do not retain heat very well and as at about this time the parents start to leave the chicks for long periods to go foraging for food, they are liable to chilling. This is especially true if the weather is cold and damp or the clutch is a small one.

When there are still unhatched eggs a chick lies so that its relatively huge, almost tortoise-like head is propped up by a shell. When all have hatched the chicks lie so that the head of each is supported by being laid upon the neck of the next chick. From the gentle cheeping noises it appears that chicks are fed several times an hour. As they get to be about eight days old, the feet begin to color, the feather tracts can be just made out, the eyes start to open, and the voice acquires a different harsher, almost angry, tone. Because of the very rapid rate of growth, a chick can be half its final weight at one week of age, and because some parents start the incubation with the first egg, the very youngest chick frequently can be

An adult male opaline cockatiel. The only trace of its former "pearled" condition is the faint stripe on the shoulder. Photo by Brian Seed.

Opposite:
Judging by color pattern alone, this opaline cockatiel could be either a female or immature male, but it could not be a fully adult male; a fully adult male would have moulted its opaline plumage and become a basically grey bird. Photo by Brian Seed.

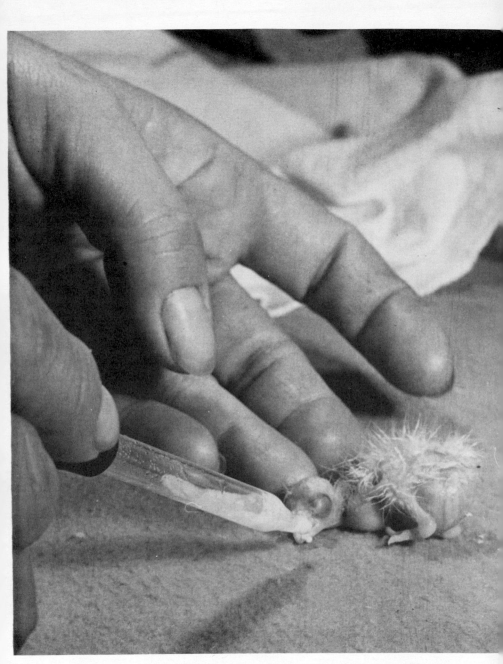

The baby cockatiel being dropper-fed here is less than twelve hours out of the shell. At this very early stage of development the babies are best looked after by their parents. Photo by John Rammel.

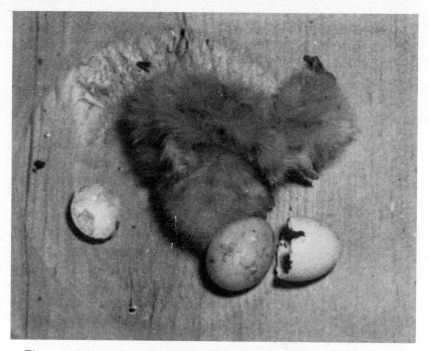

These chicks have hatched in a bare nest box; at this stage of their development one of the greatest dangers to them is chilling, and they *must* be kept warm. Photo by Louise van Der Meid.

completely hidden under a pile of massive bodies, despite which it will still be fed. The tiny cheeps of the very young seem to be particularly alluring to the parents, who assiduously search out the beak of any crying chick from the enveloping pile of bodies.

The eyes first open as mere slits and after a few days become wide and seeing. Now when the chicks are disturbed, instead of being quiet or giving the food-soliciting cheeping noise, they raise the tiny quills of their crest and threaten by rocking from side-to-side. As they rock they hiss by forcing air suddenly from the mouth. This rocking and hissing are extremely contagious, so that even the "blind" young of three or four days old join in. If chicks are regularly disturbed they often begin to hiss when they hear someone approaching. Hearing this, chicks in other boxes also take up the din.

At about ten days the parents first start to leave the

This opaline has an attractive pale yellow background color. Photo by Brian Seed.

Opposite:
Opalines showing a lack of
lacing on the breast. Photo by
Brian Seed.

chicks unattended for some of the day, and this is one of the indications that the chicks are ready for permanent marking by putting rings around one of their legs. The other indications that they are ready for banding is that their legs are becoming pigmented while the skin of the body shows signs of the emerging pin feathers. For perhaps three or four days a chick's foot is of such a size that a suitable ring can be just slipped over it onto the shank of the leg and remain fixed. By the time the chicks are more than twelve or thirteen days old this banding may become impossible to do. If the chicks are too young then the rings simply fall off. Banding is done by slipping the ring over the first three (the longest) toes up over the ball of the foot to lie on the scaly shank of the leg, but with the small hind toe still imprisoned. The little toe is eased free by using the tip of a matchstick shaped to a point.

Rings for this purpose can be obtained from advertisements in the "cage-bird press" or from petshops. The inside measurement of the rings is 5mm, which has been found to

Banding young birds. The rings are stored on the closable wire visible at left. Photo by Wide World.

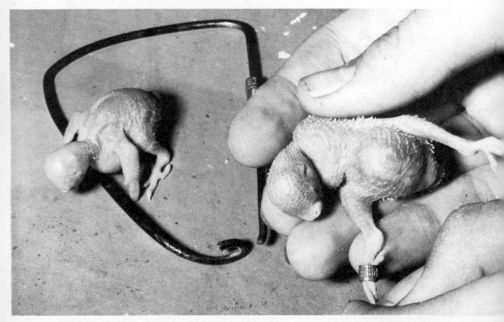

be the correct diameter to flip over a young bird's foot, but is too small to be removed except by cutting it off from the leg of an adult.

It is impossible to run a stud of any breed of animal without having some foolproof system of identification. The accepted method with birds is done with a flat bracelet of aluminum upon which various markings can be embossed. The ring can be inscribed with almost any code system, but as the space is limited, it usually gives the year, the initials of the breeder, and a number. The number is different for each chick. The rings can be in plain aluminum or anodized in some bright color, a different color for each year.

The exact system used by the author is one that tries to give the maximum of information and yet requires no recourse to a diary or notebook to check the facts at some later date. The rings have the date (for example, 77), then comes the breeder's initials (G.A.S.); if it were wished to show that the chicks were the result of crossing, say, Mr. Brown's bird with Mr. Smith's, the initials could be BXS. Following the initials come the numbers. If the first pair of parent cockatiels is known as "pair one," the second "pair two" and so on, the rings are bought from number 11 upwards. Therefore the first chick of the first pair that is banded is number 11, the second 12, the third 13, etc., and the first chick of the third pair is 31, etc. If more than nine chicks are reared from a pair, then the numbering can be 111, etc.

The nest gets dirtier and dirtier as the chicks grow because the parents practice no sanitation whatsoever. At about three weeks, or perhaps a day or two afterward, the chicks begin to climb up to the nest entrance to view the world and beg to be fed. The parents sometimes may even feed them from the entrance. Any time between 28 and 35 days they will have flown. An occasional chick may wait a few days longer, but if they take six weeks then there is something wrong with the feeding or the chicks. Once they leave the nest the chicks return randomly and may use the box as a roost for up to a week. In most cases it will be found that just about at the time that the chicks begin to fledge the hen will start laying her next clutch in the same box. Even though

A male opaline at first moult; the opaline (pearled) pattern is rapidly being replaced by solid grey plumage. Photo by Brian Seed.

A very nice pair of lutinos. Photo by Brian Seed.

This closeup of young cockatiels shows the typically enlarged crop of well-fed youngsters; these babies have just been spoon-fed by their owner. Photo by John Rammel.

Above and opposite:
One of these lutino cockatiels
(the bird farthest from the
branches in the photo above and
uppermost in the photo
opposite) is especially lacking in
yellow pigmentation, but it is not
an albino. Photos by Brian Seed.

these eggs can become somewhat soiled and lay upon the refuse of the first youngsters, they usually hatch and rear good chicks. If the parents allow time it would, of course, be better to clean the box up between rounds.

If egg laying starts well before the chicks leave, the chicks can get badly chewed by both parents. Sometimes the male bird alone does the chewing. In such circumstances it is he, and not the hen, who is wanting to start the nesting cycle once again. In this case the next group of eggs may be delayed for some time after the chicks have left.

The feathers are mostly chewed from the head and back of the chicks and very seldom are the flight, tail, or belly feathers affected. There are several ways of stopping this mutilation of the chicks, although it must be said that the need does not always apply, for the chicks usually leave the nest shortly after the pecking starts. Some have suggested spraying the chicks with vile-tasting sprays sold expressly for this purpose. They may work in some cases. The most satisfactory methods are either: 1) make the nest-box no longer attractive as a nest site by removing the top and letting in full daylight; 2) the best way is to take the youngsters from the nest. They can then be fostered, hand-reared, or (and this almost invariably seems to do the trick) put into the shelter. This latter method works only if the floor of the shelter is high, for the parents seem not to like feeding chicks if they are at ground level. Curiously, young parrots when taken from the nest in this way do not panic and spread over the floor but group in one spot. Nor do they usually leave the shelter until their allotted time of fledging arrives. The parents usually immediately stop pecking them once they have left the nest area, but if they hang about the nest they may again be feather-pecked.

No matter how badly the feathers of the young are mutilated, they still seem to in time grow into perfect plumage. But to do so must be a drain on the chick's body reserves, and the bleeding which may occur in bad cases can be very weakening. In other parrots, as a preventive for this feather pecking, a second nest-box usually entices the hen to lay her second round in that and the male continues feeding the first

This young cockatiel is enjoying the best of all possible worlds: a good feeding and the warmth of its owner's hand. Photo by John Rammel.

Above and opposite:
A fine pair of cinnamons bred by British cockatiel fancier Jim Rice; the male lacks the grey pigmentation in the head and neck area. Photos by Brian Seed.

Young birds still being fed by their parents know how to get their parents' attention; here one baby is giving the food-begging cry. Photo by Dr. Gerald R. Allen.

After hearing the food-begging cry, the male regurgitates food from its crop and prepares to feed the hungry baby. Photo by Dr. Gerald R. Allen.

With its wings held away from the body, the chick takes the food from the male. Photo by Dr. Gerald R. Allen.

An adult pied hen. Photo by Brian Seed.

An adult normally colored hen. Photo by Brian Seed.

brood. But as male cockatiels have to share in the incubation, this practice may not work, the more so as hen cockatiels usually persist in using the same nest-box.

A fledged chick solicits to be fed by lowering the crest and bobbing the lowered head with a whining noise. The wings are slightly drooped but neither quivered nor flapped. It might be three weeks before a chick, after leaving the nest, becomes entirely independent of its parents for some food.

Young birds can be extremely wild. In their fright they can cut themselves on the wire, especially upon the head, but these wounds leave no after-effects. As tame birds are so much more pleasant to have than wild ones, they ought to be tamed. The best way is to start young by bringing all young birds, once they have become independent, into a busy room. There they become very tame and docile. If the birds are later intended for show purposes or, perhaps, for pet birds, this taming is almost obligatory.

The fledged chicks, once they are independent, may be left in the parents' aviary; however, they can soon become so sexually precocious that they begin to show an interest toward the nest-box. This and the courtship display and calling of the young males can lead to fighting and, in any case, cause noticeable tension in the parents, who come off the nest. It is better, therefore, to put all the youngsters from the different pairs into one large holding aviary. Remember that overcrowding or rather the stresses of overcrowding can reduce the resistance to disease.

Problems in Breeding

NUTRITION

It ought to go without saying that before a chick can hatch from an egg the egg has to contain enough fats, protein, carbohydrates, vitamins and minerals to make the chick. As it grows, eventually to become independent of its parents, the chick will demand even greater amounts of these nutrients. Unfortunately, for it is too often expected of them, if the parents have only seed and water it will be difficult to raise a brood. Analysis of the usual food seeds reveals that they are deficient in several essential items including the amino acid lysine, the vitamins A, D, B-two, and B-twelve, and the minerals calcium and sodium. Nevertheless, despite this inadequacy it is a common experience that certain pairs, and more particularly the older birds, will sometimes lay eggs and raise their chicks on such a simple fare. The question is how they achieve this miracle, for on the face of it this is a near impossibility.

They manage because, poor though this diet is, the needs of a non-breeding cockatiel, unless it is molting or suffering from a disease, are even more frugal. Thus, before breeding, they can lay down some body reserves of certain of these essential dietary factors in "anticipation." Nevertheless, it must always greatly tax the parents to rear a clutch, as the rate of withdrawal from their bodies of the substances that are deficient in seed can so easily exceed their availability. Indeed, the body's stored reserves may become so depleted that the parent cockatiel is unable to withdraw further amounts except by drawing on its own body tissues, damaging itself. Protein and many minerals cannot be stored except as functional parts of the body, and a loss in these results

Baldness of the head can be caused by feather-plucking among the birds, but it also is an inheritable defect. Photo by Brian Seed.

Opposite:
An adult male of the normal wild-type coloration. Photo by Brian Seed.

Cuttlebone, taken during all periods of the year, is attacked with special vigor during the nesting period. Photo by Dr. Gerald R. Allen.

in wasting, debilitation, inability to molt correctly and the resistance to disease processes is reduced. Certainly it is a common experience that unless the diet is fortified in some way the parents will become increasingly lackadaisical about their brood and they frequently stop all reproductive behavior, becoming listless.

The loss to the parents of these substances results because every time that they regurgitate food from their crops to feed the chicks it is sticky with saliva and digestive secretions. These substances are, compared with the grains of seed, proportionately rich in protein, minerals and vitamins. And this is why green food, water soluble vitamin and mineral supplements, and best of all, bread dipped in milk ought to be given to all pairs of breeding parrots, together with cuttlebone to replace the constant leaching of "body goodness."

SEXING COCKATIELS

Although the differences between an adult male and an adult female are so obvious that it would be almost impossible for anyone not to notice, it can be very difficult indeed for the person not very well experienced with cockatiels to sex them before they have molted into an adult plumage or to sex some of the mutation color forms. If two birds are of the same sex they can be housed together for all time, in the most perfect of conditions, and still be unable to raise any youngsters. Yet, despite the obviousness of this statement, pairing together of birds of like sex is one of the commonest reasons for parrots' failure to breed. There are always voice and behavioral differences between the sexes of cockatiels, but to notice these might take more time and attention than the average person can manage. Therefore we shall restrict our discussion entirely to visual differences.

The adult male "normal" cockatiel should not be difficult to distinguish, for he has a yellow head, but the differences that we shall mainly concern ourselves with are the pigmentation of the primary wing feathers and the tail feathers. The male has no yellow marks whatsoever on these feathers; they are completely dark grey or black. Both sexes (when

Netting a wild cockatiel without damaging it is a tricky operation even when the aviculturist is equipped with a bird net. The object basically is to approach the bird without alarming it (above) and place the net near the bird in such a way that it flies into the net so that it doesn't have to be caught in mid-flight. Once in the net, the bird should be discouraged from flying out by the presence of a restraining hand over the opening. Photos by Brian Seed.

immature) and adult hens have a chain of yellow blotches to the primary feathers and a broad reticular network of yellow in the tail.

These quite clear differences are not shown by the males until they have undergone their first molt. Cockatiels may not molt until they are as old as nine months or they may do it as early as three months. It largely depends upon when they were hatched, for they tend to molt in the late summer or early autumn. Birds hatched in the early months of the year molt much earlier than those hatched in autumn or winter. The pattern differences in the feathers between the sexes depend upon the level of the male hormone testosterone circulating in the blood. If there is little or no testosterone circulating then the growing feathers fed by that blood take on the female type, or vice versa. Fortunately it is not necessary to wait for the natural molt to take place, as once male chicks are about three months out of the nest they are mature

Comparison of the head structure and coloration of a mature male (left) and female cockatiel of normal (wild-type) coloring. The male has a light-colored head against which the cheek spot stands out clearly; although the female also has the cheek spot, the darkness of the surrounding plumage makes it less immediately obvious. The male also usually has a larger and fuller crest, but this latter character is not completely reliable as a sex indicator. Photo by Miceli Studios.

Down feathers from a young cockatiel. Photo by Dr. Gerald R. Allen.

The arrangement of the feathers of the wing as viewed from above (upper photo) and below. Photos by Dr. Gerald R. Allen.

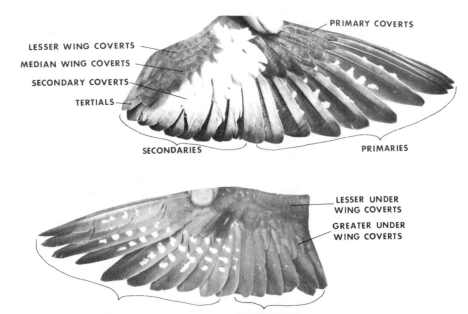

PRIMARY COVERTS

LESSER WING COVERTS

MEDIAN WING COVERTS

SECONDARY COVERTS

TERTIALS

SECONDARIES

PRIMARIES

LESSER UNDER WING COVERTS

GREATER UNDER WING COVERTS

PRIMARIES

SECONDARIES

Comparison of primary wing feathers (from left to right) Major Mitchell cockatoo, rose-breasted cockatoo and cockatiel. Photo by Dr. Gerald R. Allen.

enough to be able to grow the adult male feather pattern.

To sex immature birds of three months of age and over they are caught in a net and a single flight feather is pulled from the wing. An outer tail feather may also be taken. From practical experience it is the fourth primary feather from the tip of the left wing and the outer left tail feather that are removed. Before pulling, the feathers are first examined to make certain that the quill is fully hardened. At this age it would be remarkable if it were not. If the quill is hard the feathers are then given a short, sharp tug and they come out easily enough. About a month after this the young cockatiel is again caught and the wings and tail re-examined. Except in the lutino, the fourth primary and the lateral tail feather will have been replaced by a much darker feather than the other feathers of the body. If it is a male, then yellow spots will be lacking on these feathers. If a female, then they will be present. The loss of spots applies equally to the lutino.

However, the rise in male hormone levels does not depend only upon age and this feather-plucking method of sexing may not be quite 100% reliable if the chicks are stunted with malnutrition, have been ill, or are reared at an unfavorable time of the year. Within these limits it is most satisfactory. If doubt exists, the next adjacent feather should be plucked out at the time of re-examination. When the replacement for this has regrown (in another month) the characteristics it shows should be completely reliable.

With the pied cockatiel this method of sexing is not necessarily always possible because the primary and tail feathers so frequently lack any black pigment. Likewise the head of both sexes, when they lack black pigments-exactly as with the lutino mutation-are so alike this often cannot be used to distinguish them. What makes it more complicated is that the mutation for piedness, as well as producing the harlequin patches, also causes in both sexes each pale flight feather to have a large yellow splotch.

A careful examination of even the most well-marked pied should show that there are still a few normal grey primaries or some naturally colored tail feathers. Even if there is but one of either, this ought to be enough to sex the bird.

Gentle palpation of the bones in the pelvic area of the bird can be useful as an indicator of sex (the pelvic bones are wider apart in the female than in the male), but this method of sex determination requires experience. Here it is being used by Mrs. Kathy Novak of Novak's Aviaries.

In practice it will be found that it would be a most exceptional pied that lacked such "sexing" feathers. It is a great pity that such secondary feathers cannot be used for sexing purposes, for they are far less often affected by the pied factor. This is because although most hens will have barred secondary feathers, some do resemble males by having them clear of all yellow pigment. Worse, some males have them spotted!

The only absolute method, the one that leaves no doubts whatsoever as to the sex of a chick, even before it reaches some degree of maturity, is to use as the male parent a sex-linked color mutation. A cinnamon, lutino, or laced male paired to a hen of any color other than that of the male will always give hen chicks that are the same color as the father, while the male chicks are of normal grey appearance. For example, a lutino male mated to either a normal, pied, cinnamon, laced, or red-eyed silver hen will have lutino daughters and sons that are normally colored. This method of sexing becomes complicated only when the male and female are "split" for other colors. Even if they are and other colors can make their appearance, this method still may have an absolute 100% reliability. What is more, by using a lutino male the sexing can be very prompt in demonstrating gender, for the chicks can be sexed the day that they hatch or even in the egg. If a very bright light is shone through a partially incubated egg, a male will be seen to have a black eye and a female a pink one that cannot be differentiated from the rest of the tissue.

GENERAL FACTORS

Some moments of thought should always be given as to which cockatiels to breed from, even if the pair are only intended to be used as foster parents to a more valuable color mutation. A poor breeder or inadequate parent will take approximately the same food and will demand exactly the same housing as will a good bird.

The majority of cockatiels are reasonably tame, but sometimes an occasional bird is found that is excessively shy. Such a nervous creature hearing or seeing someone ap-

166

Adult lutinos are more difficult to sex than adults of the wild-type color, but chicks produced from the mating of a lutino male to a female of any other color will be easy to sex even at a very young age. because the male's color will be transmitted to only his female offspring. Photo by Manolo Guevara.

Very young cockatiels like this one keep the crest erect almost continuously; this is a distinct departure from the behavior of adult birds, which keep the crest depressed most of the time.

proaching its aviary is certain to give the cockatiel alarm call. It is bad enough if they leave their own nests, but the frantic calling frequently brings even the more sedate birds from theirs. Over the years these nervous birds generally improve and make good parents, but it may not be until they have caused considerable disappointment from cracked eggs, chilled chicks and general mayhem in the colony.

If some hand-reared animals are brought up with little knowledge of their own kind, their mental make up becomes distorted towards their own species. The tame animals come to identify themselves with humans rather than with their own kind. Finger-tame male cockatiels are known to court their owner and other people, and yet drive away female cockatiels. This extreme behavior is exceptional, and most tame cockatiels make good parents. A bird that is completely or partly humanized may be at least partially "cured" by housing it with a few other cockatiels as reasonably far away from human contact as possible and leaving it very much alone for a month or more. This method reduces the otherwise inevitable competition between cockatiels and humans for its attention. When paired up again, keep the bird in a place where it does not have too much human contact. Once they successfully start to breed, this caution about contacting the bird can be withdrawn.

It is not good to breed from particularly small, deformed or badly feathered birds even though it is very likely that such defects will not be inherited by their offspring. Small hens tend to lay small eggs and the larger the egg, within reason, the greater its viability and the ultimate size of the chick. Other things being equal, the weight of an adult bird is very much dependent upon its hatching weight. It has been said, for example, that the various bantam or miniature poultry breeds are evolved not, as might be thought, by selecting for small-sized parents, but from incubating only the very smallest of eggs. Then, again, small adults have proportionately less body reserves, are less well able to withstand stress, and are not able to cover or keep warm as many eggs. Defects and deformities may be indicative of having at some point suffered from an illness. Certain diseases of birds, and particularly salmonellosis and psittacosis, could be passed from seemingly healthy parents that have recovered from these illnesses and are now carriers to their chicks.

Try not to breed from very young birds, as it will frequently cause disappointment because of their incompetence. What may sometimes be taken as an incompatibility between a pair of otherwise seemingly suitable parents could result from one or both may still be able to contact their previous mates by sight and sound.

It is something of a nuisance to have what can only be termed as oversexed cockatiels. Perhaps it is because natural selection operates to give these birds, even in the wild, all the breeding characteristics of a long-domesticated species: a continual breeding cycle, very high fecundity, a near-promiscuous sexual activity and an ability to breed despite enduring what, to other animals, would be extremely adverse conditions of housing and management. Whatever the explanation, the sex hormone level of some cockatiels appears to be, on behavioral grounds, abnormally high.

Hens so affected will persist in laying their second clutches well before the first brood is reared. Unwanted eggs may be fostered off or destroyed, but their removal does not always stop the hen bird harassing the chicks. "Oversexed" males may attack chicks while they are still in the nest or after they fledge and can be most annoying. Sometimes these males become so belligerent that they waste no opportunity to fight with any adjacent pair of birds and may not, because they are so occupied, bother to brood or look after their family.

The opposite condition, that of "undersexed" birds, can be just as annoying. The pair may refuse to nest or incubate or may look after their chicks in so lackadaisically that the eggs never hatch or the chicks die in the nest. Such greatly disappointing birds may be influenced by the weather, the time of year, by illness, or by being frightened (especially by mice or cats) through the night. It has been a general experience in temperate climates that if summers are drier than normal cockatiels are not much interested in breeding. The molt or heavy infestation with parasites puts great strain on the birds, the more so if the diet is only just adequate.

The position of the nest-box in the aviary may be important in some cases. Cockatiels certainly do not appreciate an enclosed environment such as an aviary built in the shade of a tree. In some cases they simply may not have noticed the entrance hole to the box. A seemingly non-breeding pair belonging to the author immediately investigated and soon laid inside a box that had, until it was shifted to a more open position, previously not even been looked into. The entrance hole ought to always face into the flight and be just next to and slightly above the height of one of the perches, so that the birds cannot help seeing it each time they settle.

THE FEMALE

Although seemingly normal, some hens appear to be unable to ovulate. They begin the usual nesting pattern except that they spend day after day continually sitting in the nest but never actually lay. Ultimately, of course, they may do so, but it has been found by Marriott that if one of these non-laying hens, which incidentally are almost always young birds, is given another cockatiel's eggs to foster, she and her mate will accept them as being theirs. The substitute eggs should be added at the rate of one or two a day and not be given all at once. After they have reared these foster chicks, almost invariably the hen lays perfectly normally afterward.

The opposite also happens that a hen continues to produce egg after egg without seemingly ever finishing her clutch. Frequently such a hen does not brood. Indeed, it may be the lack of brooding which instigates this condition. But even if she were to incubate, as a cockatiel can only physically cover so many eggs, most would not hatch. If this condition is not resolved, it too frequently leads to the death of the hen from the constant drain upon her body system. If the eggs are indelibly marked and the first six laid are left in the nest (the ones after six should be removed and stored or fostered) then if the hen does become broody she can be set on fresh eggs.

To more easily understand the afflictions of laying hens it is necessary to know a little of how an egg is formed. With certain exceptions, birds have a single ovary and oviduct situated in the left side of the abdomen. About the time that the hen first starts to accept the attentions of the male, her ovary begins to enlarge with developing ovarian "yolks." The ovum of a bird, when compared to that of a mammal, is relatively huge and we all recognize it as the yolk of an egg. Within the ovary of the hen cockatiel each yolk of the intended clutch is already present (but each will be in a different stage of development) just before she starts laying. The yolk of an egg is particularly rich in fat. If a hen is short of rich food, perhaps because she has to share her meals with the parasites in her intestines or because she has a most inadequate diet, then she will be able to grow very few yolks or perhaps none at all.

Two days before she lays her first egg a mature ovum is shed from the ovary and is immediately fertilized by the sperm stored in the oviduct. Most of the matings that take place between the parent cockatiels are sterile for there is no exchange of semen. But the proportion of fertile matings rapidly increases toward the time of egg-laying so that the female comes to have sperm always present in her oviduct. The sperm of parrots, once inside the oviduct, are (relative to mammalian sperm) long-lived. If the male is taken away, the hen cockatiel would, very likely, be able to lay fully fertile eggs for a week and after that time some of the subsequently laid eggs would be infertile. It might take more than a month before the hen would be unable to lay any more fertile eggs.

The fertilized egg now starts to travel down the oviduct where it has first secreted about it an elastic twisted structure the "chalaza," of thicker egg white or albumen. The chalaza supports the yolk inside the egg so that the developing chick, located as it is upon the very top of the yolk, is always upward, at the warmest point of incubation just under the body of the hen, no matter how the egg is turned. The egg white is then added to surround and embed the chalaza and, finally, a membrane. The very last part of the oviduct contains the shell glands which deposit calcium carbonate (chalk) in a layer around the shell membrane to form

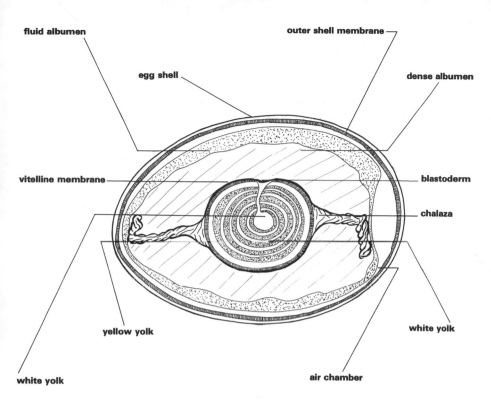

fluid albumen

outer shell membrane

egg shell

dense albumen

vitelline membrane

blastoderm

chalaza

yellow yolk

white yolk

white yolk

air chamber

The structure of a bird's egg. (After Keymer, *Bird Diseases*.)

the egg shell. It takes about a day for the ovum to get to the shell gland area and another day for the shell to form. The egg is then laid. Just before laying another yolk enters the oviduct to start on the same journey.

Sometimes (in young hens or those that are suffering from some disease) the ovum instead of entering the oviduct is shed into the abdominal cavity. Very shortly afterward the hen begins to look unwell. She forsakes her nest and sits with fluffed plumage and usually passes a thin diarrhea which pastes the feathers of her vent with a sticky whiteness. This condition is known as egg peritonitis and is incurable.

If the hen bird lacks sufficient vitamin D or had no opportunity to eat quantities of calcium-rich food during or before laying, she will be unable to deposit calcium carbonate to make the normal egg shell. The hen will then either lay a soft-shelled egg or, if the calcium salts in the blood become depleted, show those symptoms known to bird-fanciers as egg binding. Egg binding means that the egg is stopped in its passage down the oviduct, for the oviduct becomes paralyzed when the levels of blood calcium fall, so the egg can move no farther. The egg-bound hen becomes increasingly shocked, leaves her nest, becomes indifferent to disturbance and sits huddled in a sleeping posture. Usually after but a day or so she was so worsened that she dies. There are methods of relieving a hen so distressed.

The standard treatment for egg binding is warmth. This succeeds by reducing the effects of shock. Putting liquid paraffin or other oils into one end of the bird or the other will make the bird more ill, and even if it does not have that bad an effect, the oil cannot possibly get into the oviduct where it is supposed to lubricate the egg and send it moving once again. Egg binding is a complaint that should never arise, for it is perfectly preventable; but should it happen, then a one milliliter injection of 30% calcium borogluconate given under the skin of the neck and then spread by massage will usually be effective within half an hour or so.

Calcium will only get to be transported about the body if there is a sufficient amount of vitamin D present to mobilize it. Therefore even if such things as cuttlebone and old mortar—the standard means of feeding calcium—are fed and the hen has an inadequacy of this vitamin then she will not be able to absorb sufficient calcium for her requirements from the bowel. Nor, having absorbed calcium, will she be able to store it in her bones as reserves against the needs of egg-laying. And, equally, it will be difficult to mobilize what reserves of calcium she does carry back into the blood, into the shell glands and then deposit it onto the shell membrane as an egg shell.

In the summer it is fair to accept that the bird will be able to make enough vitamin D from the sunlight that falls upon its body reacting on certain skin and feather fats; but in northern Europe and northern North America the winter days are not long enough, nor the sun bright enough, to make the vitamin. To avoid egg binding, domestic cage and aviary birds, including the cockatiel, ought to have vitamin

174

D fed them during the winter. Some of the vitamin D will be stored in the bird's liver for use later in egg laying. The so-called "water soluble" vitamin D, found in various commercial "vitamin supplements," is far, far less effective than cholecalciferol or vitamin D-3.

Vitamin D-3 is easily provided by using cod liver oil soaked seed. Mix about a teaspoonful of the oil to a pound of canary or canary-millet mixed seed. The oil is poured onto the seed and stirred with an old spoon kept specifically for this purpose (cod liver oil taints cutlery with a persistent

Cod liver oil as a food additive to supply needed Vitamin D is available at pet shops everywhere.

smell of fish). The next day the oiled seed should be thoroughly mixed by hand and only after this second mixing should it be fed. Most of the cod liver oil will be left on the husk. But the cockatiel only eats the kernel of the seed! Yet, even so, enough will be absorbed by the bird husking the seed in its bill. Such oil-soaked seed is fed from the months of November until early March in the Northern Hemisphere. After that provided that the bird has access to sunshine, it is not needed and, in any case, cod liver oil might go rancid with the summer heat and become harmful.

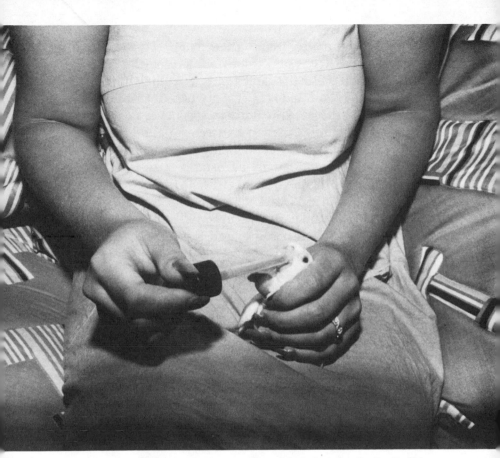

Vitamins can be given to the birds by soaking their foods in vitamin-enriched fluids or can be directly administered by eye-dropper. Photo by Dr. Herbert R. Axelrod.

Opposite:
A view into one section of a commercial breeding operation. The flight, at right, has plenty of window area and extends all the way to the ceiling; individual breeding pairs are caged at left. Photo by Leslie Overend.

LOSSES IN THE NEST

When the embryo contained in an egg dies at a very early stage, the egg is said to be "addled;" if the embryo dies later, so that it is clearly identifiable as a chick, it is said to be "dead-in-shell." Addled is misused when describing an infertile egg, for in this case the embryo has never begun to grow. "Bad eggs" are those infected by bacteria and are usually the consequence of the egg shell being cracked or because the shell is porous. Eggs may get cracked if there is not sufficient litter in the base of the nest to prevent the eggs from rolling against each other. Cracked eggs also happen when the parents are wild and easily disturbed. The cause of egg shells being porous is often obscure and the incidence may differ from year to year. Among the factors that may be considered to have some relevance are sub-clinical poisoning by chemical insecticides, either from being directly applied to the bird and its nest box or from farmers spraying the seed during its growth. Insecticides to be used on birds or in the nest-box ought to be pyrethrum-derived or based upon other vegetable substances such as derris or rotenone. D.D.T., B.H.C., or any man-made synthetics should not be used. Perhaps reduced levels of vitamin D may also be responsible for some cases of porous shells.

Death of the embryo and addled eggs can sometimes be the consequence of an indifferent pattern of incubation, usually because one of the parents is less broody that it might be. The early death of the embryo, giving rise to addled eggs, is usually ascribed in text-books of poultry management to an insufficiency of various vitamins, proteins and minerals, but most particularly to lack of vitamins of the B series. Inbreeding and so inadvertently introducing recessive genes that are responsible for debilitating, deforming or even killing the chick at an early age may also be considered.

Dead-in-shell is usually said to be caused by the nest-box being too dry. Desiccation makes the incubating egg lose too much water to the atmosphere. The chick is then weakened and cannot break out of the egg. However, this theory may not always be true. Several times during their incubation parent cockatiels soak themselves with water. This dousing

The egg tooth is still visible at the tip of the upper mandible of each of these cockatiel hatchlings. Photo by Dr. Gerald R. Allen.

seems to be the natural way of moistening eggs and, after all, cockatiels naturally use very dry holes in trees. It is found that dead-in-shell is most common in the colder months of the year and is aggravated by bad parents. Those parrot breeders who use a moist nest-box filler, such as peat, have just as high an incidence, if not higher, as those who give no form of moistening agent. Dead-in-shell is likewise more common in draughty or thin-walled boxes than in well-made substantial ones. It is also noticed that when some eggs do give chicks, the incubation for these has been a day or two longer than expected. Although desiccation may be responsible, it seems that chilling or undue cooling also is largely involved with dead-in-shell.

Sometimes it comes as a pleasant surprise to find that there is one more chick in a nest than there were eggs. Such extra chicks come from one of the eggs having been double-yolked. The chicks, in such cases, are not necessarily any smaller than the others; however if they are very much smaller then the probability is that they will die. As the incidence of double-yolked eggs can be selected for in domestic poultry, it is best not to breed from any birds that show this or any other form of reproductive disorder. Most "infertilities," from the considerable evidence taken from other animals including birds, are extremely likely to be strongly inherited.

Inevitably, some disaster or other will give the breeder some surplus cockatiel eggs. If the eggs cannot be fostered off with another pair, rather than destroy them they can be put into an incubator. It is more convenient to have a group of chicks hatch together rather than one every other day, so the eggs have to be stored until the clutch is complete before they are incubated. Eggs must be stored in a cool place where the temperature lies between 40° and 60°F (4° - 20°C). They must be turned at least once a day during their storage. Whatever is going to be the subsequent fate of "orphaned" eggs, it may avoid problems if they are marked in some way with an indelible felt-tipped pen. Mark the date, details of the parentage, or whatever information could be needed later. A ballpoint pen cannot be used for it will go straight

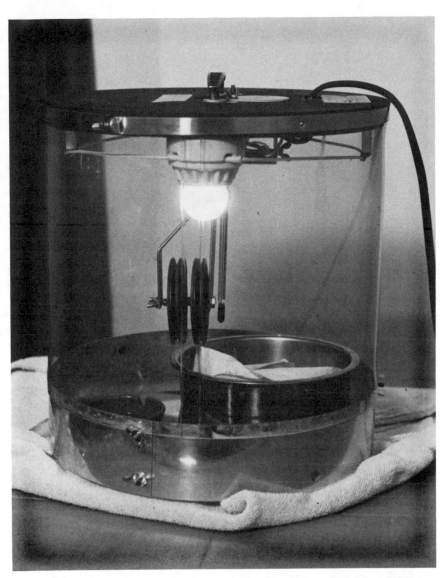

A mechanical incubator. In this unit the heat is provided by an electric light bulb. Photo by Manolo Guevara.

through the egg shell. Pencil is out if the eggs are going to be put under a bird, for the marks will rub off. To avoid making the eggs a mass of hieroglyphics, it will be found that Roman numerals using dots instead of strokes prove best. The very best artificial incubators are those in which the air is circulated by a fan and have some form of humidity control. It is particularly nice if the eggs can be mechanically turned as well, for they really ought to be turned several times a day. This can be an easily forgotten chore in the midst of one's daily business.

The temperature of incubation should be set at 100° F (38° C). When the eggs are mechanically turned, do not—as the makers suggest—stop the rotating mechanism in the last two days of incubation. It has been found that their hatchability will not be affected by the turning. With the "damp wick" of the incubator reading 91° F (70% water vapor saturation), hatchability has been found to be as good as it would have been had the eggs been incubated by the best of parent birds.

It is a very good principle to examine all incubated eggs for fertility, whether in an incubator or under the parents, when they have been set for five or six days. It is a waste of a bird's time and energy to sit upon eggs that cannot hatch. In an incubator such eggs can explode and contaminate chicks that hatch from other eggs with various potentially harmful organisms. These can enter their bodies through the wet umbilicus as the rotten eggs can be a very powerful source of spores of the mold *Aspergillus*.

If the eggs of a sitting cockatiel are infertile and both parents seem to be otherwise perfectly normal, the clutch might well be replaced with fertile eggs from another pair. These foster eggs must have been incubated for an equal or a longer time, for it is found that when incubating birds have set for a variable number of days over the normal incubation period, they desert the clutch and start again. The fertile pair, having lost their eggs, usually start to lay within less than two weeks—indeed, sometimes in as short a period as four days—and their second clutch will usually also be fertile. If the infertile pair are permitted to lay again it is

182

very likely that they will lay another clutch of useless eggs.

A freshly laid or an infertile egg when held in the palm of the hand looks almost as if it were translucent. When put between a source of light and the eye, it appears to be a diffuse color. After four or five days of incubation, the egg now looks to be a duller, almost grey-white. It seems opaque and, when held up to the light, it will cut out light and appear to be darker. If the light source is strong and cannot get to the eye save through the egg, as can be done by fitting the egg into a slightly smaller hole in the top of a dark box inside which is a light bulb, then a dark blob radiating red "spider's legs," the growing embryo and its blood supply, can be made out. The only real way for the novice to become absolutely certain in his judgment of whether an incubated egg is fertile or not is to make a regular practice of examining eggs in the nest. It is far from difficult and after but a little while even the most cursory glance can give all the necessary information as to whether the egg is alive or not.

If there is any uncertainty about whether a chick is in the egg, never break it to find out, as it is almost certain to contain one. If eggs have not hatched after three weeks of artificial incubation, or 24 days after the last egg was laid with natural incubation, open ONE and if this is a dud then another and so on. Never decide to break all the eggs in one glorious smash. If a living chick is found stop breaking any more. Dead chicks cannot move and there is no hemorrhage on opening. The state of development of the live or dead chick inside its broken shell will give a very good idea of how much further time is needed to incubate the remainder of the clutch.

THE CHICK

Probably the most dangerous time in a chick's life is the first three days after hatching. Death can be due to many causes including such accidents as being trapped inside its own hatching egg by the egg getting inside the shell of an earlier hatched egg. This is one of the reasons for removing egg shells from the nest. Others get infected through the yolk

The remains of eggs from which some babies in the clutch have already hatched should be removed from the nest before all of the other eggs have hatched, because sometimes part of the shell that contained a hatched chick can cover an unhatched egg and prevent the unhatched chick from leaving the shell. Photo by Louise van Der Meid.

184

sac cord or are misshapen or deformed in some way. The most common cause of loss is that they are not fed by the parents. Frequently this happens because they are weak from cold and are too inert to plead for food. These chicks if taken into a warm atmosphere such as an incubator and artificially fed for a few days, can then be returned to the parents provided that other chicks, or eggs, are still present.

Between breeding rounds the nest-boxes ought to be cleaned well and perhaps rinsed with a mild disinfectant. If it can be arranged that the sun can shine directly into the inside of the box, this is probably the most beneficial way of drying after cleaning the box. Sawdust or any other material intended to be used as a nest-box filler must be fresh and dry. Aspergillosis, a fatal respiratory disease, has been observed by the author in two nests of cockatiel chicks in which garden compost had been used as bedding.

Another of the more critical periods is when the chicks are ten days or so old and they are just beginning to quill up. This is when the parents tend to leave them alone for part of the day. On several occasions dead chicks of this age have been shown to have died of a ruptured liver caused by one of the parents clumsily dropping onto it instead of climbing down the wire ladder inside the box. This is why boxes are not built too deeply. Most frequently, however, post-mortem examination shows that the liver and kidneys are noticeably enlarged and very pale, indeed almost creamy pink in color, while the body contains much excess fat. Such chicks, like the surviving ones, are particularly well-grown and well-cared for. An exactly similar appearance in growing poultry is called the "fatty liver and kidney syndrome," or FLKS for short. The exact cause may vary but it is found in fast growing poultry on high energy rations, particularly when the diet is poor in biotin (one of the vitamin B's). FLKS has not been found in nestling parrots when the parents were liberally fed with green food.

Sometimes cockatiel chicks have rickets. Rickets is a bone disease of the young. The two main causes of rickets are the lack of sufficient vitamin D or calcium in the diet. In rickets the growing bone is softer than normal and bends

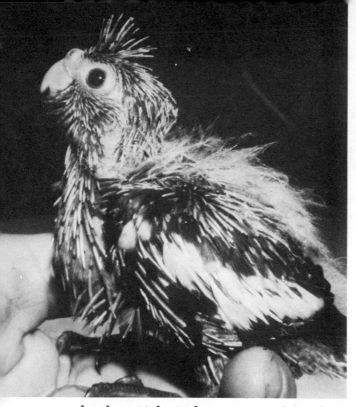

The pinfeathers of a young cockatiel are very well illustrated in this view. Photo by Dr. Gerald R. Allen.

under the weight and movement of the chicks to give distorted limbs. This is most apparent in the legs. Affected chicks sometimes cannot climb out of the box when their time of fledging arrives. Others, the worst affected, die as they begin to feather. Some that do leave can fly only a very little distance before crashing to the floor. If placed on a perch they topple off because they cannot grip with their feet. When held in the hand the joints of ricketty cockatiels are noticeably thicker than normal and the legs are seen to bend inwards. The least affected chicks will grow slightly better with time; the worst examples are better killed. On autopsy it will sometimes be found that the legs are so soft that the bones can be bent before they break and the skull so thin that it is dimpled by very slight finger pressure.

Rickets is preventable. Parent cockatiels often consume a whole cuttlebone a week when they are feeding chicks to provide the chicks with calcium. Milk will give both calcium and vitamin D, and one or two slices of bread steeped in milk will be eaten daily by a pair with a large brood. In at least one instance rickets has been attributed to the parents feeding the youngsters almost entirely on oats. Oat seed can contain high levels of phytin (anositol hexaphosphate). This substance binds to calcium in the bowel of the bird and prevents it from being absorbed.

HAND-REARING

Sometimes the only way of saving chicks will be by hand-rearing them. This is not quite as tedious a task as might be imagined. Parrot chicks have very large crops and therefore, to start with, only need feeding four or five times

To the inexperienced eye, baby cockatiels—and the ones shown here are still babies—don't appear much different from mature cockatiels. Photo by Dr. Gerald R. Allen.

a day and later, when they are beginning to feather, but three times. Admittedly they might benefit if the meals came slightly more frequently than this. Apart from food, the very young chicks need to be kept warm until they are three weeks old. If too cold, they will not feed with any enthusiasm nor can they digest their food efficiently; they could pine away and die or, at best, grow slowly. For the first week the chicks might be kept at about 95° - 100°F (35° - 38° C), dropping to 80°F (27°C) at two weeks. When too warm the chicks will pant and take on a rich pink color. In this case drop the temperature by 5°F (3°C).

A nest made from a small cardboard box and lined with paper napkins is ideal to house them in at first. If an incubator is not available for the cardboard box then a place in

Development of cockatiel chicks is swift. This chick is 24 days old. Photo by Dr. Gerald R. Allen.

This cockatiel is 32 days old and ready to leave the nest. Photo by Dr. Gerald R. Allen.

an airing cupboard will do. Another method is to put the small cardboard box, containing the chicks, inside a somewhat larger box in the bottom of which is a hot-water bottle filled with water slightly higher in temperature than blood heat. The whole can be draped with a towel or polystyrene tiles to retain the heat, and it ought to remain warm for eight hours or so. Ventilation is necessary, of course, and the paper napkins are replaced as they get soiled.

Because the parent cockatiels feed their young on canary, millet, sunflower seed, etc., it is often assumed that the person hand-rearing them also has to do so. Thus we get advice to husk grain in an electric mixer and then blend this with certain other foods and altogether make a rather tedious, time-consuming business of food preparation. This is in

189

no way necessary for we have several really excellent preparations for feeding human babies that are based upon ground vegetable grains and which are further supplemented with minerals, milk protein and vitamins. These "cereal baby-foods" are compounded to give a complete diet and may be mixed with either water or milk. No extra minerals or vitamins should be added although carrots and fruit or vegetable juices might be used instead of water and milk. With very tiny baby parrots the mixture should be made rather more moist than for older birds. Both the food and the mechanical means of feeding it, spoon or syringe, must be quite warm. If not it will be found that the baby cockatiels will not swallow.

Like other parrots, the baby cockatiel does not gape wide for food. It is normally fed by the parent taking a light hold with its bill on that of the chick while its tongue spoons regurgitated food into the chick's partly opened bill. While it is being fed the chick chirrups and vigorously bobs its head. The person hand-feeding a cockatiel chick cannot therefore simply push food into an open maw but has to work the food in through a narrow opening which does make the feeding take just a little longer than it might.

The cockatiel chick is held in one hand with a paper tissue to wipe its face after the meal. The beak is touched or, perhaps better, slightly squeezed between two finger tips. This should make the chick bob its head and make swallowing movements. If it does not, then try putting the food forcibly, but gently, in at the angle of the bird's mouth. The means of holding the food will differ. Some use a hypodermic syringe without a needle, while others have found that a child's paint brush quickly scooping the food directly off a small saucer is wonderfully efficient. A teaspoon with its sides crushed in a vise to bring them closer together, used either directly to pour the food into the bill or push it off this with a child's brush, is most useful.

The crop of a chick in the nest is not always full; nevertheless, the aim in hand-rearing should be not to let the crop remain empty for too long. There is no need to wake during the night to feed the chicks, provided that the crops are well-

Very messy but very effective—babies abandoned by their parents or taken from them so that they can be hand-reared and thus made more amenable to taming will get a lot of food all over themselves when fed from a spoon, but the important thing is that they'll get plenty of food *into* themselves as well. Photo by John Rammel.

filled in the evening. The amount of light allowed to reach the chicks can be increased once their eyes start to open, and they soon come to recognize the person feeding them and will chortle for food when they see the syringe or spoon used to feed them. If the weather is very dry it can be beneficial if the chicks are given fresh water to drink after they have been fed. The chick will, if thirsty, often take water when it will refuse food.

The chicks must be handled during the rearing to make them as tame and confident as possible. The beak must be kept clean, for if food is allowed to become impacted on its surface it might cause ulcers or deform the mandibles. As with chicks in the nest, the feet must be frequently examined to make certain that they are not clogged with dry feces.

The most trying period in hand-rearing is often the weaning. Young birds that are artificially reared often seem to be more tardy in learning what food is than are their naturally reared brethren. The pap necessarily used in rearing, if spilt, is not as attractive to a chick as would be the spillage of grain kernels lost by the parent. Once the chicks are five weeks old they must always have some seed in the cage with them, especially a millet spray or some green food. After hand-feeding, a grain of sunflower can be offered in the fingers. They often take this and mouth it before putting it down. But this slight practice does attract their attention to grains. Putting in another young cockatiel who has already learned to eat for itself will get them started quicker. Eventually all hand-reared chicks give up begging and take to self-feeding, even if it may seem that yours will prove one terrible exception. By the time that they are seven weeks old they should be eating by themselves.

Blue and gold (yellow) macaw, *Ara ararauna.* Photo by A.J. Mobbs.

Regardless of its color variety, a cockatiel remains basically the same interesting and intelligent pet. Color and pattern have parts to play in satisfying owners' tastes but have no effect on the personality and behavior of the bird. Photo by Harry V. Lacey.

8: A Guide to the Color Forms

INTRODUCTION

It seemingly took more than one hundred years before one of the many tens of thousands of captive-bred cockatiels appeared that was very different in color from the rest. This bird, as we have read in the introductory chapter, was a harlequin or pied. It would have been perfectly possible for the normal-looking parents of this pied to have continued producing other pieds in the approximate ratio of one pied to every three normals. Likewise the offspring of this pied when mated back to their grandparents, the original pied parent, or between themselves, would have produced yet more pieds.

Such a sudden change in the appearance from the parent-form is called a "sport" and if a sport can be perpetuated through subsequent generations it is called a *genetic mutation*.

By no means are all color changes in birds due to genetic factors. For example, if parrots are fed on a diet of sunflower seed with no extras, as they molt some feathers may grow that are yellow or white instead of the usual green or black. Similarly if the food of a pink flamingo has no carotenoids, which are plant-derived coloring substances, then it will molt out to have white feathers and pale legs. These two color changes are nutritional and reversible. Once the diet is corrected these birds in their subsequent molts become normally pigmented. The young of these nutritionally deprived birds, assuming that during their period of rearing they are given a satisfactory diet, will not have the abnormal coloring of the parents

Pesquet's parrot, *Psittrichas fulgidus*. Photo by A.J. Mobbs.

Opposite:
Green-winged king parakeet,
Alisterus chloropterus.
Photo by A.J. Mobbs.

The majority of color mutations result from the bird having a genetic error, a defect, somewhere in its body's chemistry. This makes it unable to synthesize the usual pigments. Such color changes as these mutations create are, therefore, the consequence of a biochemical deformity. It would be most exceptional, though certainly not impossible, for a color mutation to be the result of a process "added" rather than "subtracted" from the bird's already existing metabolism.

As with so many mutations, these color mutations are RECESSIVE to the DOMINANT wild-type. This simply means that when cockatiels with these novel colors are paired to normals the offspring look exactly like the wild-type with no hint that one of the parents had a different color. Even though the wild-type may dominate completely, the mutation is not lost. When these young are mated with each other or back to the differently-colored parent, they will produce some of the visual mutants for themselves. In avicultural literature the normal-looking birds that carry the mutation are known as SPLITS, which is much less of a mouthful than the geneticist's *heterozygotes*.

YELLOW AND BLACK

The wild-type or "normal" cockatiel has but two colors: yellow and black. The general grey feather results from a "mingling" of black and white or black and yellow. When a feather that would otherwise be grey lacks yellow, it is black. Likewise, if a feather that should be grey has no black, then it is yellow. Where it lacks both of these colors, the feather is white. As yet no one seems to have given the yellow color a name. It has sometimes wrongly been called a carotenoid pigment. Carotenoids are taken directly from plant tissues and require little modification by the birds.

However, the yellow of parrots is seemingly quite distinct from this and is completely synthesized by the parrot. It may be exclusive to this order of birds. Despite a strong desire to call the pigment "*psittacin*," it shall be referred to as "yellow." Yellow must be fairly easily synthesized by the cockatiel and other parrots from the most simple of diets, for

198

The breeding of cockatiels for improvements in their color—or for the development of completely new color forms—can add a fascinating depth to the bird-keeping hobby and can be very profitable as well. Photo by Harry V. Lacey.

Black lory, *Chalcopsitta atra*. Photo by A.J. Mobbs.

Opposite:
Swift parrot, *Lathamus discolor.*
Photo by A.J. Mobbs.

nothing seems to be able to be fed, or to lacking, to affect its intensity. It may seem odd, considering the enormous variety of colors available to parrots, that their oranges, reds, blues, purples and greens are formed of the same black and yellow.

The blue of parrots is not a pigment but results from a layer of colorless and extremely minute, indeed submicroscopic, rods running over a central core of the black pigment. Blue is the consequence of light striking this refracting layer, and the green comes from "mingling" the blue with yellow. There is good reason to assume that red and orange are simple chemical modifications of yellow, and they will be treated as if they were the same.

YELLOW

If a large sample of male cockatiels is examined, it will be noticed that there is much variation in the amount of yellow present on the head, both between birds and in the individual. The yellow is at its deepest around and above the bill (the face) and the forepart of the crest. It then fades as it approaches the patch of orange on the ear-coverts. The palest birds have no yellow behind this "cheek" patch and this part of the head is white. We have previously noted how the young cockatiel, from the time that it hatches and for some week or so afterward, is covered with a thin yellow down and how, if several chicks are examined, it will be found that they can differ considerably in their depth of yellow. The intensity of yellow in the chick ultimately is that of the adult: deep yellow chicks make deep yellow adults, and vice versa.

The relationship between the orange of the cheeks and the yellow of the face is very close. Examine several males and it will be seen that most of the darker yellow birds have an occasional orange-colored feather scattered about the face. The darker yellow the bird, the brighter the orange and the more frequent these feathers.

In an interval of four years it has twice been possible to closely examine a talking, ten year old male normal cockatiel. Unfortunately the owner will not breed from it, nor allow anyone else to try, which is a great pity, for it is quite

A clue to the eventual depth of yellow coloration in male cockatiels can be gained by examining the babies in the nest. The babies that will eventually have the deepest yellow coloration as adults will have the deepest yellow color in their down. Photo by Brian Seed.

the most uniquely-colored cockatiel that has been seen by the author. The face and anterior part of the crest are quite a distinct orange-yellow, thus partly confirming the opinion that yellow and orange are akin. The belly and chest feathers have so great a density of yellow pigment that it has almost obscured the black contained in the feathers, making them appear quite a bright yellowish-grey. The wing-bar, which we know is usually white, is a very rich deep yellow, and so is the entire head.

Goffin's cockatoo, *Cacatua goffini.* Photo by A.J. Mobbs.

Lesser sulphur-crested cockatoo, *Cacatua sulphurea*. Photo by A.J. Mobbs.

The above description shows that the yellow pigment can be found at different concentrations in different cockatiels. Experience proves that cockatiels can be selected for their richness of yellow, but the genetics is complicated by the seemingly high number of genes involved. My present opinion is that four shades exist. The commonest is the palest of all. In the "normal" the low "dose" of yellow gives males with a great deal of white behind the ear patch. In lutinos this low "dose" of yellow gives a near-white bird. And despite the factor for pieds intensifying yellow, the harlequin patches are white, while in cinnamons and red-eyed silvers the color is a very dilute greyish, silvery brown. The opaline or laced is not particularly striking either. The rarest combination of genes for yellowness produces the deep yellow, such as described for the normal male above. These give bright yellow lutinos, very pretty opalines, the cinnamons and red-eyed silvers with a rather nice yellow suffusion. The intermediate combinations of genes for yellowness give two stages between these extremes.

As so much of the beauty of the mutations next to be described is greatly enriched by the intensity of the yellow background, selection should always be made with this in mind. In the nestling the deepest yellows can be noted by the shade of the down. The number of genes involved and the compound effect of their massed numbers mean that selection is best done by eye rather than by a simple adherence to genetic principles and theory. The golden rule (the pun is intended) is: *reject all pale birds for breeding, whatever other merits they might have!*

THE LUTINO ("Albino)

The lutino was the second mutation to be established. Unlike the pied, this bird immediately took the avicultural world by storm because it was so like a miniature white cockatoo with a pale yellow breast and an almost white body, tail and wings. The head and crest were primrose yellow, and both sexes had a brilliant marigold-red patch on the cheek. The dull, drab grey duckling that is a normal cockatiel had, by this mutation, become a most beautiful white swan.

The lutino cockatiel was one of the earliest color mutations and remains one of the most popular color varieties now being bred. Photo by Brian Seed.

Yellow-tailed (black) cockatoo, *Calyptorhynchus funereus funereus.*
Photo by A.J. Mobbs.

Salmon-crested cockatoo, *Cacatua moluccensis*. Photo by A.J. Mobbs.

By far the most successful mutation in terms of numbers bred and for beauty is undoubtedly the lutino. It was a complete tragedy that these pale yellow cockatiels were first described as "albinos" because it left people satisfied with what were, after all, rather insipid-looking near-whites. The avicultural term of "lutino" is used for that special type of albinism in which, although completely unable to synthesize melanin, the bird can still produce yellow and red pigmentation.

Fortunately, some of the more perceptive of the European breeders put some effort into getting increasing amounts of yellow into the plumage, but the issue became confused because these improved lutinos began to be known as "primrose," "yellow," or "real lutinos," as if a totally different mutation had been conjured up.

The present world stock of what must be by now more than ten thousand (including those in Australian aviaries; remember that Australians have not been allowed to import birds, except from neighboring New Zealand, since the late 1940's) are descended from a single seemingly normal cock bird owned by Mr. Cliff Barringer of Florida. Mr. Barringer had bred fourteen perfectly normal youngsters from a pair of what he had always taken to be perfectly normal grey cockatiels when, in the next nest of two youngsters, he found that he had one with pink eyes. This surprise occurred in 1958. The following year the parents produced two more of these unique birds. Strange as it must now seem, no attempt seems to have been made to breed from the normal nest mates, for approximately half of the seemingly normal sons of this parent male would also have bred lutinos. Indeed, it took two years for Mr. Barringer to produce the first male lutino by mating one of the lutino daughters back to her father.

It seems that the following year Mrs. E.L. Moon, who used to be the curator of the Florida Parrot Jungle, acquired the nucleus of Mr. Barringer's stock and it was from her subsequently named "moonbeams" that the lutino cockatiel eventually spread throughout the world. Mrs. Moon wrote a delightful book entitled *Experiences with My Cockatiels* (TFH Publ.).

The mutation for lutino is common to several species of

parrot. The black, brown, purple and blue colors of parrots depend upon the presence in the feathers of the black granular pigment called melanin. Where the melanin is covered by a layer of submicroscopic rods that refract light the feather looks blue; if a superficial layer of yellow covers this refractive layer, then the feather—because it is both blue and yellow—appears to be green. In cockatiels, Pesquet's parrot and the cockatoos the refractive layer possessed by other parrots is not developed and the yellow and black, working together, give the grey appearance.

If the bird cannot synthesize melanin, then the yellow pigments remain to make it a lutino and not an albino. An albino is pure, clean white with no other colors on any part of the body whatsoever. The ability of the body to form melanin is notoriously liable to be altered by some genetic mutation. There can hardly be any tame species of animal that has not been known to have albino, pied, red or even completely black individuals such as white crows, sparrows, ginger cats, albino guppies, black panthers, white mice, etc. These sports owe their very frequency as well as their considerable variation to the biochemical fact that the black granular melanin is only made after a chain of separate biochemical processes have taken place. Each intermediate process in the chain requires a distinct enzyme. It is believed that genes are ultimately responsible for making enzymes. Therefore genetic mutation affecting any one of several genes will affect the production of melanin. Depending on the gene each mutation *could* give a slightly different, as well as the same, effect on the finished melanin. This appears to be so. All the known mutations of cockatiels affect the formation of melanin, but the end result is different in all cases. Thus, we have fallows, opalines, cinnamons, lutinos and pieds.

Lutinos are, by definition, sex-linked (see the next chapter for greater detail), which means that a male lutino must have had a lutino mother. But a lutino hen obtains her color wholly from her father. The color of her mother is immaterial. So lutino hens can be bred from lutino males or split lutino males, but a male lutino must have a lutino or a split lutino father as well as a lutino mother.

Eclectus parrot, *Eclectus roratus.* Photo by A.J. Mobbs.

Kea, *Nestor notabilis.* Photo by A.J. Mobbs.

The inability to make melanin in a lutino is not confined to the feathers: the feet, skin and eyes are pink. The pink color of these tissues is that of the blood flowing through them. It has been reported that some lutino cockatiels have black eyes. This is very curious indeed. Eventually it might be shown that such black-eyed lutinos have eyes that have suffered from hemorrhage or some other damage so that the resulting scar-tissue interferes with the normal passage of light through the eye. Or that such birds possess some modifying gene, or genes, that pigments the eye. Whatever the explanation (and it will take a microscopical examination of a dead cockatiel's eye to find out), the so-called "black-eyed lutino" is most definitely not a separate mutation from Mr. Barringer's lutino.

To function normally, the inside of the eye has to have a heavy layer of melanin to completely soak up the superfluous light entering the eye. The lutino cockatiel must have very poor vision because its eyes have no menalnin. It can manage well enough in poor light; however, on a very bright summer day it can become quite blinded. The shelter and the nest-box will give them protection from the bright light, but young birds after fledging may spend most of their time in flight, and permanent damage might be done to their vision. It is wise to keep young lutinos indoors or in shaded aviaries, particularly in bright weather.

It is perfectly straightforward to pair a lutino (for it is a sex-linked recessive in its inheritance) to a normal cockatiel as there is no chance of "losing" the factor in an uncertainty about whether youngsters will bear the gene or not. Nevertheless, the early breeders seemingly paid slight interest to increasing fertility, vigor or depth of yellow by outcrossing. Indeed they often did quite the opposite. For example, someone quite early mated lutinos into a line of cockatiels that were genetically bald. Baldness, fortunately, is dominant in its inheritance and can be eliminated very simply by avoiding breeding from any affected bird. When two bald birds are paired together some of their progeny will have two genes for baldness. Instead of having, as with the single gene, a small patch without feathers on the nape of the head post-

214

Mrs. E.L. Moon and one of her bird friends, a sulphur-crested cockatoo. Mrs. Moon was a pioneer breeder of both cockatiels and other bird species in the United States. Photo by M. Kruger.

erior to the crest, these have a most unsightly bare nape sometimes as large as the end-joint of the thumb.

The early lutinos arose in a strain that had a low quota of genes for yellow and were not always fertile. Some of this infertility was because the males had an inborn defect of behavior that made them uncertain as to which direction to face when pairing with the hen. Such a male would mount the hen and then turn first this way and then that and then lower himself to pair facing quite the wrong way around. Most eggs, consequently, were infertile.

Hyacinth macaw, *Anodorhynchus hyacinthinus*. Photo by A.J. Mobbs.

Vernal hanging parrot,
Loriculus vernalis.
Photo by A.J. Mobbs.

Violet-necked lory,
Eos squamata.
Photo by A.J. Mobbs.

217

THE OPALINE, LACED, OR PEARLED COCKATIEL

What is in a name? A lot in this case, for by analogy to a budgerigar, this mutation must be that for opaline. However, the West German who bred this described it as pearled (*gesperlt*). The same pattern of having a dark area surrounding a paler center is called "laced" in flowers and birds as, for example, laced pinks and laced Polish bantams. The pearled cockatiel is now frequently called "laced" in England. Because the nape of the head, the mantle, and the upper wing coverts are the only feathers affected, it does seem to replicate the opaline of budgerigars.

The opaline cockatiel first occurred in West Germany in 1967 or perhaps in 1968, for exact details are hard to find. But rumor has it that the same mutation was found in Belgian birds the year after. The feathers affected by this mutation are unable to produce melanin in the central portion of the vane. This results in a pale patch on either side of the feather shaft. The effect is somewhat variable in how any individual will be affected. In the better examples a narrow border of dark grey margins a white or yellow feather to give a really handsome scalloped pattern. Others, and unfortunately it seems the majority, have less melanin loss to the feathers and the bird has a marbled appearance. In the very worst examples the cockatiel looks spotted or smudged. When the basic yellow background color is a deep yellow then the contrast with the grey makes them especially pretty. These have been called "gold-laced." When the yellow is very weak they are known as "silver-laced." This does not mean that there are two distinct mutations.

Youngsters from the same nest are rarely exactly alike and parents that have produced splendidly marked youngsters one year may not subsequently repeat this success. Two well-marked parents have no greater chance of producing well-marked youngsters than would two ill-marked birds.

One feature that to some appears curious and to others perplexing is that male opaline cockatiels, when they molt for the first time, lose their lacings. This happens because one of the secondary sexual characteristics of male cockatiels is to lay down a higher density of melanin than do females or im-

218

There is a great variation in the quality of the markings of the opaline, or pearled, cockatiel. Photo by Brian Seed.

Red-fronted conure, *Aratinga wagleri*. Photo by A.J. Mobbs.

Tui parakeet, *Brotogeris sanctithomae*. Photo by A.J. Mobbs.

Left: Patagonian conure, *Cyanoliseus patagonus. Right:* Blue-crowned hanging parrot, *Loriculus gagulus.* Photo by A.J. Mobbs.

matures. The extra black melanin of maturity therefore obscures the pearled effect, but not quite completely, for if close examination is given it will usually be found that the shoulder feathers look paler, as if they were slightly soiled with excrement. It has been reported that in some cases old pearled males regain some of their laced feathers. It does seem very likely that selective breeding would reduce the amount of melanin deposited in the feathers of adult males. Mrs. E.L. Moon selectively bred for paleness most successfully. Until that time arrives, male opaline cockatiels will always be something of a disappointment.

Another curiosity is that split males can be picked out from normals because they have pale streaks of feathers under the wing near the shoulder joint, giving a mottled effect.

Because the opaline is another of the sex-linked mutations, it is easy to breed in quantity. However, it is particularly important to always fasten permanent closed bands to the legs of these birds, when chicks, because of the difficulty in distinguishing adult male opalines from normal grey cockatiels.

CINNAMON OR ISABELLE

In 1968 Mr. van Otterdijk discovered that a Belgium bird-fancier had long been breeding cinnamon cockatiels. Cinnamon is another common mutation of birds and, like the lutino, is always inherited in a sex-linked manner. Cinnamon is called *Isabelle* in European countries other than Britain. Melanin is still produced but the granules produced are brown, not black, and may be slightly smaller than are the granules in the normal black form. The cinnamon melanin, because it does not absorb so much light, gives the feathers a pale, brownish-grey color. If the yellow background is intense then the cinnamon cockatiel is a most beautiful pale foxy-brown. With a light yellow background to the feathers, the bird is a very pale cafe-au-lait (coffee-with-milk).

As we have seen, adult male cockatiels acquire more melanin than hens or youngsters and therefore the darkest shades of cinnamon are seen in the adult male. There is,

Cinnamon cockatiels. Cinnamon cockatiels are attractive but not generally in as good supply as the other well established cockatiel color varieties. Photo by Brian Seed.

Ruppell's parrot, *Poicephalus rueppellii*. Photo by A.J. Mobbs.

Yellow-streaked lory, *Chalcopsitta sintillata chloroptera*. Photo by A.J. Mobbs.

however, considerable variation, probably because genes affecting the intensity of grey exist in cockatiels. Certain exceptional birds are said to be almost as light as lutinos in pigmentation, whereas others are but a few shades lighter than the usual grey.

PIED OR HARLEQUIN

The pied was the first mutation to be recorded. Visually this is extremely variable in the effect that it produces, and there is no means that might be used to select for an increased effect. In other words, parent birds with very well-marked plumage stand no greater chance of producing nicely patterned youngsters than would the mating of the most ill-marked specimens. Pied cockatiels are so variable that an exceptional bird might be almost lacking any normal feathers and therefore would appear practically white, while another may have only a few white feathers and be otherwise grey. These extremes are very, very rare indeed. Those several hundred seen have some pied patches to the head, usually on the crown and cheeks. The rump, too, is usually affected, as are some of the flight feathers and parts of the tail. The second effect of the pied gene is to cause those flight and tail feathers that are whitened to carry a broad spread of yellow pigment rather than the usual barring. This yellow is not lost when the males mature. Sometimes it is only the head that is left with sufficient grey with which to determine the sex. In this case females may still have the orange ear patches obscured by the grey.

Unfortunately, and this has happened with practically all of the mutations, no one thought to record their early history. What is certain is that it was already established by Mr. D. Putnam, of San Diego, California, some time before 1951. After the death of Mr. Putnam his stock was acquired by Mr. Hubbell, who carried on breeding them. Coincidentally, as Mr. Putnam was working on his strain Mrs. R. Kersh was building up another. It is not known whether these mutations were entirely disconnected, but is is reasonable to assume that both stemmed from the same mutation of some years previous that has been passed, unnoticed, from parent cockatiel to offspring although never producing any pieds for lack of the necessary inbreeding. All we know is that Mrs. Kersh's foundation bird was bought from a pet store. It does appear that most of the European pied cockatiels came from Mrs. Kersh's stock.

The early history of breeding for pieds suggests an extremely high degree of inefficiencey or of sterility among the birds, as in the first twenty years extremely few had been bred. One likely explanation is that there is always a tendency to select for color in autosomal recessives by mating pieds to 'split' pied birds. In practice this invariably brings close inbreeding. The mating of close relatives is likely to introduce other genes that may interfere with viability or fertility. Whatever the reason, the world total of pieds, in 1968, may well not have exceeded one hundred, and they sold for a minimum of $100 in the States and for approximately twice this sum in Europe. See West, 1968, for details.

The most perfect pied would have a complete symmetry to its patches. This could well be almost impossible to achieve. Likewise the pale areas are at their most attractive when they are clear cut with a sharp demarcation between the grey and white. The deeper the yellow background, the more attractive the pied.

The three previous mutations (opaline, lutino, and cinnamon) were sex-linked; the pied is not. Before a pied can be produced both its parents must carry the factor, and this mode of inheritance is more common than sex-linkage.

RED-EYED SILVER (Fallow)

This is the latest of the color forms to have been reported, and some see it as being as attractive as the lutino. It is of a light silver color. Strangely, if feathers of the cinnamon and red-eyed silver are examined in the hand little difference, if any, can be made out between them, and yet the birds are quite distinctive.

The reduction in melanin is sufficient to make the eyes appear to be as pink as they are in the lutino. Because in the budgerigar such pink-eyed cinnamons are called fallows, this might be the better term for them.

226

Both the intensity of yellow background color and its regularity of dispersal throughout the feathering are important in determining how good a pied cockatiel is as a representative of its color variety. Photo by Brian Seed.

This mutation is still quite novel and, being inherited in an autosomal manner, considerable inbreeding has taken place. Whether it is this inbreeding or because the gene has effects other than those on the feathers, there is said to be a very high incidence of blindness or very defective vision in silvers and their fertility is also low.

SILVER GREY

In the early 1950's at approximately the same time that the pied cockatiel was making its first appearance in America, an occasional "silver grey" was reared in New Zealand. Unfortunately there seems to have been either a complete lack of rudimentary genetic knowledge or of simple husbandry, for the strain appears to now be lost. From the written account, these were singularly beautiful birds. It is not, of course, improbable that this mutation was that later known as cinnamon or even the black-eyed silver. We may never know.

WHITE NAPE

This is really quite an insignificant mutation for it merely causes the bird to produce a few white feathers to the back of its head. It is dominant in its inheritance, for any parent with such a white nape will have some offspring that also bear this feature. By some curious quirk several strains of pied also have a gene for producing white napes. Therefore, by pure coincidence, many split pieds will have a white nape. Pied is completely recessive and does not mark the split form in any way. The presence of a white nape is irrelevant to piedness.

THRUSH-CHESTED

This is another dominant mutation with only a very slight significance. The affected cockatiel has some of its chest and belly feathers with a reduced amount of melanin, so they give a speckled chest to the bird. As the opaline mutation does not pearl the feathers of this area, a more attractive bird is produced by combining these two mutations.

FURTHER MUTATIONS

It is amazing that so many color mutations have arisen in so short a time in the cockatiel, all of which affect only the production of melanin. Mutations likely to convert the yellow background color into a deep orange-marigold, now only found on the cheeks, are unlikely and yet far from improbable. There are several cockatiels that have some orange-red feathers scattered over the head and body, indicating that such a change can take place, but it would most likely take further mutations rather than skillful pairing to get such a desirable bird.

The one mutation that is guaranteed to turn up at some time is the one that will completely eradicate the yellow and orange pigments. Such a mutation is as common in parrots as is that for producing lutinos. It normally produces blues, such as blue budgerigars, Quaker parakeets, Indian ring-necked parakeets and lovebirds. The cockatiel will not, because of its cockatoo feather structure, be blue but will be black. If this gene for eliminating yellow is introduced into the lutino, then it will give a bird devoid of all color and produce a "true" albino of virgin whiteness.

Several people have, supposedly, produced green or blue cockatiels. In the course of their evolutionary history the cockatoos have lost the ability to incorporate within their feather structure the refractive layer possessed by most other parrots. Unless this layer can be restored, blues and greens cannot be made. Not that reverse evolution cannot take place. Two other features once selectively "lost" by cockatiels have made an exceptional reappearance. One adult hen has been noticed to have regained the ability to beg the male to feed during courtship. Another cockatiel has been seen using its foot for grasping and holding, something that has been impossible for the vast majority of cockatiels for a long period of time, even though it is common among other parrots. The return of the refractive layer to the feathers, to give them a blue or green appearance, may require a far more sophisticated association or mutation of genes to get this "reversal of evolution" than does the re-acquisition of courtship feeding or being able to use the foot as a hand.

The normal (wild-type) coloration in cockatiels is dominant as a genetic characteristic to the other colors so far known among cockatiels. Photo by Harry V. Lacey.

9: COCKATIEL GENETICS

INTRODUCTION

From personal experience, as well as from reading the queries posed in cage-bird journals, it seems that many bird breeders have little or no knowledge of simple genetics. Among the questions asked are: "What colored youngsters will result if cockatiels of different colors are paired together?"; "Can a cockatiel be split for two or more colors?"; "Can a cockatiel be both pied and lutino and, if so, what color will it appear?"

Such questions will be answered, but before doing so in greater detail it might be best to start by giving a straightforward list of various matings. After the list, which will not be complete owing to the enormous numbers of possible matings, an elementary account of the principles of inheritance and a broad definition of the words used will follow. By making the explanations as simple as possible it ought to enable anyone to work out breeding charts for any crosses they may wish to make.

VARIOUS MATINGS

LUTINO male (or female) **X** lutino female (or male) = 100% LUTINO OFFSPRING.

LUTINO male **X** NORMAL female = All female chicks are LUTINO and all male chicks are normal in appearance but are actually SPLIT LUTINO.

NORMAL male **X** LUTINO female = NORMAL females and SPLIT LUTINO males.

LUTINO male **X** PIED female = male chicks normal in

appearance but split for both LUTINO and PIED. Female chicks are LUTINO but are also split for PIED.

LUTINO male **X** SILVER female = Males normal in appearance but split for both LUTINO and SILVER. Female chicks are LUTINO but are also split SILVER.

LUTINO male **X** OPALINE female = Male chicks normal in appearance but split for both LUTINO and OPALINE. Female chicks are 100% LUTINO.

LUTINO male **X** CINNAMON female = Male chicks normal in appearance but split for both LUTINO and CINNAMON. Female chicks are 100% LUTINO.

SPLIT LUTINO/SPLIT PIED male **X** LUTINO female = 50% males will be LUTINO and half of these will also be split for PIED. The other 50% of the males will seem normal but will be split for LUTINO and approximately half of these will also be split for PIED. Of the hens, 50% will be LUTINO and half of these will also be split for PIED. About 25% of the hens will be perfectly normal and the remaining 25% look normal but are split for PIED.

PIED (male or female) **X** PIED (female or male) = 100% PIED.

PIED (male or female) **X** NORMAL (female or male) = 100% split PIED.

SPLIT PIED (male or female) **X** SPLIT PIED (female or male) = 25% PIED, 50% PIED, and 25% NORMAL.

The list could go on, but it would be very repetitious. Cinnamon or opaline can be substituted for lutino in the above, or silver for pied. But rather than look at tables it is perfectly simple to work them out for oneself once a few simple genetic points are understood.

A MUTATION is any abnormality, be it for color or anything else, that can be passed from a parent to some members of succeeding generations.

A GENE is the unit of inheritance. A particular gene will henceforth be referred to by the name which describes its main effect. So we will have a "lutino gene" or a "cinnamon gene" instead of the circumlocutory "gene for producing a lutino effect."

PURE-BRED. A cockatiel will be said to be pure-bred for some color mutation if, when mated to a similarly-colored bird, all the offspring they produce will be the same color as the parents.

RECESSIVE and DOMINANT GENES. If a pure-bred color mutation is crossed with a pure-bred cockatiel of a different color, it will be found that their resulting offspring will be the color of one of the parents or the wild-type grey, or the male chicks will be the wild-type grey and the female chicks the color of the father. The color that has apparently disappeared is said to be RECESSIVE, and the color taken by the chicks is said to be DOMINANT.

As an example, if a pied cockatiel is mated to a normal cockatiel, then all the offspring will look perfectly normal. But the recessive color is not lost for each youngster. Even though it is not visually apparent, they still carry the gene. This is proved because when mated back to cockatiels pure-bred for the color or when mated amongst themselves, they will be parents to more of these visual recessives. For example, if these normal-looking youngsters (from a pied parent mated to a normal cockatiel) are mated back to pieds, then they will have approximately 50% of their youngsters normal-looking (they are in fact also carriers of the pied gene) and the other 50% will be pied. Such carrier birds are, in avicultural language, called splits.

CHROMOSOMES. Genes are carried on string-like bodies known as chromosomes. Each cell of the body, except for the reproductive cells—the sperm and the egg cells—always have matching pairs of chromosomes. These paired chromosomes are the autosomes. Because the autosomes are paired, the genes that they carry are also paired. As well as the autosomes, each cell carries sex-chromosomes which determine the sex of the bird. These are dealt with later.

If a gene is represented by its initial letter then a pure-bred pied can be shown as **pp**. The "p" is in lower case to indicate that it is a recessive gene. Because they are dominant to pied, the normal genes are shown as **PP**, the capital letters representing their dominance. The split condition is **Pp**.

The sex-cells, the sperm and the ova, contain only one chromosome from each pair of sex chromosomes. When these combine to produce the fertilized egg, the number of chromosomes is restored to the double state. Each parent therefore gives the chick one from each pair of chromosomes, or, as in our example, one of the genes for color. Therefore if we mate a normal **PP** to pied **pp**, the offspring get a **P** from one parent and a **p** from the other. Therefore they are **Pp**, split for pied.

When a split pied **Pp** is mated to another split pied **Pp** the parents can, in the sperm or ovum, give either a **P** or a **p**. These combine at fertilization and eventually yield a chick which contains **PP, Pp** or **pp** genes. This is shown in the following diagram:

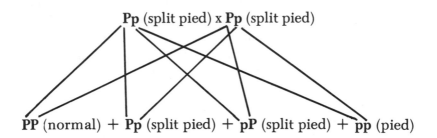

Pp (split pied) x **Pp** (split pied)

PP (normal) + **Pp** (split pied) + **pP** (split pied) + **pp** (pied)

(**Pp** is, of course, identical to **pP**). From a mating of split pied to split pied approximately 25% of the chicks will be perfectly normal grey cockatiels, **PP**; 25% will be pied, **pp**; and 50% will appear normal but are, in fact, split pieds, **Pp**.

A red-eyed silver cockatiel paired to a pied may be shown in the same way. However, instead of silver as plain **ss**, we have to also show that it is normal for pied, **PP**. A silver therefore is **ssPP**. Likewise the pied **pp**, being normal for silver, is shown as **SSpp**. The cross offspring from this mating, by receiving one gene from each parent, are split for silver and pied **SsPp** but visually seem to be normal cockatiels.

234

When these split pied/split silvers are mated together the situation is more complex. Each parent again contributes but one gene of each pair. This is best shown by the chart.

MALE'S GENE CONTRIBUTION

		SP	Sp	sP	sp
	SP	SSPP	SSPp	SsPP	SsPp
	Sp	SSPp	SSpp	SsPp	Sspp
	sP	SsPP	SsPp	ssPP	ssPp
	sp	SsPp	Sspp	ssPp	sspp

FEMALE'S GENE CONTRIBUTION

Key:
SSPP = *normal*
SSPp = *split for pied*
SsPP = *split for silver*
SsPp = *split for silver and pied*
SSpp = *pied*
Sspp = *pied and split for silver*
ssPP = *silver*
ssPp = *silver and split for pied*
sspp = *silver and pied*

These results are very interesting because they show what a wide diversity can come from but two colors. Particularly noticeable is that only one in approximately sixteen chicks will be completely normal, lacking either mutation. Eight of the chicks that seem normal are split for pied or silver or both. Three are pied, and two of these are also split for silver. Three, likewise, are silver, and two of these are also split for pied. Only one of the sixteen combines both features in a visual form and is a silver pied.

Of course further silver pieds could then be bred by pairing suitably split progeny together. In practice this may be rather complicated because it would take several test matings to determine exactly the genetic constitution of each normal-looking bird (to see if it was split for any color). The offspring from the trial matings would, in their turn, also have to be test mated. This has brought us to the first dictum in breeding which is: *avoid mating a split to a split.* Pair splits to pure-breds. This way the genetic constitution of the offspring is always known.

Charts can be made of the mating. We will confine ourselves to but one: that of mating a visually silver cockatiel that is also split for pied, **ssPp**, to a pied that is split for silver, **Sspp**; or **ssPp** *x* **Sspp**

One parent's contribution of genes **(ssPp)**

		sP	sp
The other parent's contribution of genes **(Sspp)**	**Sp**	**SsPp**	**Sspp**
	sp	**ssPp**	**sspp**

Key:

SsPp = *normal in appearance but split for pied and silver*
Sspp = *pied in appearance but split for silver*
ssPp = *silver in appearance but split for pied*
sspp = *silver and pied*

From this mating only four types of young are possible. Approximately 25% will be normal in appearance although split for both silver and pied. Another 25% will be silver and at the same time split for pied. Another 25% are pied and split for silver. The remaining quarter are silver and pied.

SEX-CHROMOSOMES and SEX-LINKED MUTATIONS

There is an exception to the rule that genes and the chromosomes that bear them are always paired. Males have two sex-chromosomes and females, for the purpose of this chapter, have only one. The sex-chromosomes of the male are shown as **XX**. The female has but one X and a very small chromosome, called **Y**, to pair with it. For our purposes we shall entirely ignore **Y**, as it almost certainly carries no genetic material, and shall refer to the female condition as **XO**; that is, **X** and **zero**.

As males have two sex-chromosomes, each sperm gets but one. The ova produced by the female have only half their number with a sex-chromosome, the rest have none. Therefore, if a sperm fertilizes an ovum with a sex-chromosome, the resulting chick, because it has two sex-chromosomes, is a male. If the fertilized ovum lacks a sex-chromosome, then it will give rise to a female chick. The diagram might make this clear.

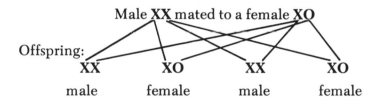

Male **XX** mated to a female **XO**

Offspring:

XX	XO	XX	XO
male	female	male	female

This is a beautifully simple way of ensuring that exactly as many males are to be born as females.

Should the sex-chromosomes carry a recessive color gene such as the lutino, then the male can be normal **LL**; split for lutino, **Ll**; lutino, **ll**. However, a hen has but one sex-chromosome and can be either normal **Lo** or lutino **lo** but cannot be split for lutino.

One of the male's sex chromosomes has to come from his mother; the female, remember, has but one, so a lutino male *must* always have a lutino mother. The opaline (laced or pearled) and cinnamon colors are likewise produced by a sex-linked mutant gene. A male, consequently, can be split for any of two sex-linked genes; for example, split for lutino and cinnamon. There is a phenomenon called *crossing-over* whereby a male could be split for three or even more sex-linked characters, but we shall ignore this complication. The doubly split birds would have a normal appearance except, of course, that split opalines have a few pale feathers on the underside of the wing near the shoulder.

A sex-linked, pure-bred color mutation male, or a male split for two separate sex-linked color mutations, can be used for sexing purposes. If a lutino, cinnamon, or opaline male is paired to a normal hen, then each of his daughters gets a sex-linked mutant gene, as do his sons. The daughters, because they lack another sex chromosomes, are the same color as the father, if pure-bred, or one of the split colors. The males, and this is why they are males, get a sex-chromosome from the mother (which is normal) and one of the sex-linked color-chromosomes from the father. Therefore they are normal in appearance even though split. The diagram illustrates this:

<table>
<tr><td align="center">**ll**
lutino male</td><td align="center">X</td><td align="center">**Lo**
normal hen</td><td></td></tr>
</table>

gives **lo** daughters and **Ll** sons.

or

<table>
<tr><td align="center">**lc**
split lutino/split cinnamon
male</td><td align="center">X</td><td align="center">**(LC)O**
normal
female</td><td></td></tr>
</table>

gives:

<table>
<tr><td align="center">**Lo**
split cinnamon
male</td><td align="center">**lo**
split lutino
male</td><td align="center">**lo**
lutino
female</td><td align="center">**co**
cinnamon
female</td></tr>
</table>

For mating a sex-linked mutation with one of the non-sex-linked (autosomal) mutations, the same principles apply. We shall use the lutino and pied as examples and consider specifically the pairing of a lutino male, **llPP**, with a pied hen, **LOpp**. The designations and chart are as before:

When dealing with a cockatiel that shows one of the colors that is recessive to the dominant wild-type coloration, you can be sure that it carries no gene at all for the wild-type coloration. These opalines, for example, can be either pure opalines or split for opaline and one of the other recessives, but they cannot carry the gene for wild-type grey coloration. Photo by Brian Seed.

Male llPP	lP
Female Lopp	
Lp	**LlPp** male split for lutino and pied
op	**loPp** lutino female split for pied

Therefore, as expected, all female chicks are lutino and split for pied and all male chicks are split for pied and lutino. If we cross, for the sake of example, the chicks we get 12 different combinations.

As before we have sixteen possible combinations. They give a normal male and a normal female. The interesting

Male **LlPp**

	LP	**Lp**	**lP**	**lp**
lP	**LlPP** male split lutino	**LlPp** male split lutino and pied	**llPP** male lutino	**llPp** lutino male split pied
lp	**LlPp** male split lutino and pied	**Llpp** pied male split lutino	**llPp** lutino split pied male	**llpp** male lutino and pied
oP	**LoPP** female normal	**LoPp** female split pied	**loPP** female lutino	**loPp** female lutino split pied
op	**LoPp** female split pied	**Lopp** female pied	**loPp** female lutino split pied	**lopp** female pied and lutino

Female **loPp**

240

two are the male **llpp** that is pied and lutino and female **lopp** likewise. Lutino completely overwhelms any production of melanin, therefore these two birds are visually lutino. It would be interesting if we knew whether the yellow in the wings is blotched, as with a pied, or barred as in a lutino. Not having seen such a bird, this is conjectural.

COMBINING THE DIFFERENT MUTATIONS

The lutino X pied mating above demonstrates how extremely pointless it is to combine a lutino with any of the other mutations, for the lutino overwhelms the mutational effects of the other genes. Crossing any of the various sex-linked mutations is equally pointless, as the females take but one from either a lutino, cinnamon or laced. The male, although split for any two, always looks perfectly normal.

However, it may be worthwhile to cross pieds with cinnamons, opalines or silvers. Cinnamons to red-eyed silvers would produce very attractive youngsters, but none have been seen.

WHAT TO DO WITH A FRESH MUTATION

Some time or other fresh color mutations are bound to arise. The person discovering these is then posed with the problem of what is the best breeding policy to take. First it has to be established that this is a genetic mutation and not just a curiosity or freak of nature. Second, the mutation wants building up into further numbers as rapidly as possible. Logically it might be better to prove its genetic foundation by mating the youngster back to one of its parents. If the mutation were an autosomal recessive then father to daughter or mother to son would give 50% of the fresh mutation. If it were sex-linked, then father to daughter would give 25% of the fresh mutation males, 25% of females, 25% of split mutation cocks, and 25% of perfectly normal females.

However, a moment's reflection shows that the parents ought to be left together. They have proved their fertility and, if it is a mutation, would produce other examples in time. Likewise chicks take time to mature and young birds are often poor breeders until they are a year old. If mated to

241

a parent this may actually delay the production of further examples. In my opinion, as well as leaving the parents together, the mutant ought to be paired to a normal cockatiel of known high fertility and the brothers and sisters mated together. Odd birds should be mated to very fertile normals. Except for the last mating, either known splits or further mutations will be produced. Subsequently, pure-bred mutations ought to be mated to normals if further examples of splits are wanted and for new "blood." Splits should always be mated back to pure-breds, trying always to avoid mating split to split. Doubtful splits can be mated to pure-breds to test their genetic constitution.

10: Disease

INTRODUCTION

Bird-keeping books invariably have a chapter on ailments and treatments. Such a strong tradition suggests that the owners are hypochondriacs about the health of their pets or that captive birds are frequently ill or are very susceptible to injury. Several species of bird, although regularly captured from the wild and offered for sale, are not suitable for aviculture. They customarily eat foods, such as insects, for which there is no good artificial substitute or, perhaps, require to be housed in an environment that does not differ too greatly from their native tropical rain-forest. But, like the other fourteen or fifteen species of truly domesticated birds, the cockatiel's captive diet is not too different from that of wild ones. Indeed, except for the actual species of seed, the domestic cockatiel's diet may be almost identical in the nutrients absorbed. Except by restricting flying, even the most bare and unimaginatively furnished aviary or cage cannot be more austere than can some of the Australian desert.

All diseases, even though they are usually attributed to a specific microorganism or deficiency of some food item, are aggravated or precipitated by stress of some kind. Stress includes all those circumstances and conditions which create disturbance or an unease in what would otherwise be a normal mental or physiological state. An animal of any kind that is perfectly well fed and housed but is unable to relax because of overcrowding will fall ill. If disease organisms are present, these will introduce a specific disease. The disease process or organism causing the disease may be treated specifically, but without also reducing stress this disease or another will again make the bird ill. Even otherwise harmless bacteria, molds or viruses can create a disease if the stress is great enough.

Pneumonia may be taken as an example of stress creating disease. Most mammals, including the reader, have present at all times in their lungs the organisms that cause bacterial pneumonia. They cause no upset and the animal is unaware of their presence. But if the body is subject to stress and the resistance of the mammal to infection is lowered, as, for example, by becoming thoroughly chilled and soaked, then these otherwise innocuous organisms rapidly build up numbers and invade the lung tissue and cause bacterial pneumonia.

Because the cockatiel's domesticated life and food are not too different from the wild, they are remarkably free from disease. Indeed, in just over three thousand post-mortem examinations of parrots of about one hundred and forty species, only twenty-one have been adult cockatiels. Another twenty-four have been nestlings. The nestlings and most of the adults came from my own breeding or from immediate friends. This is seemingly because the majority of breeders accept losses in the nest as being "natural." By far the largest number of deaths in cockatiels are directly attributable to the stresses of breeding.

INJURY AND ACCIDENTS

Captive birds sometimes suffer from broken limbs. It is really amazing how much trouble can come from leg rings. Amazing because in the sheltered environment of an aviary or cage, birds sometimes get caught by a ring getting snared over a projecting wire in circumstances that might be thought impossible. Aviary wire must therefore be well fastened down. If domesticated birds can do this, what hazards must wild birds, banded for scientific study, meet in a natural environment? The loss by post-banding accidents might, very conceivably, be the greatest cause of loss in some populations of wild birds, and any studies that do not take into account this wastage (and none seem to) must give an entirely incorrect final result. If the leg that is broken carries a close-ring, this must be cut off. This is easily performed using

244

This is the proper method of holding an untamed cockatiel for examination. The bird is gently cradled in the palm, with the index finger bracing the head and neck from behind; the thumb and its meaty base imprison the bird from one side and the remaining three fingers the other side. Photo by Miceli Studios.

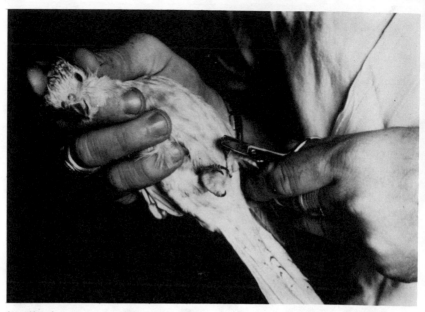

In clipping a cockatiel's claws the owner has to be very careful not to cut into the claw beyond the vein. Special blunt-tipped scissors should be used to avoid injuring the bird. Photo by Miceli Studios.

a very sharp pair of nail clippers and biting these onto the ring across its depth. The bird is held by an assistant and the operator steadies the ring with his other hand. The ring is then pulled open. If sharp nail clippers are not available, take the bird to a veterinarian.

Birds are extremely resistant to infection from open wounds. Amputation, even of the most dreadful-looking of "compound" fractures, should never be restored to until it has been proved that the limb is indeed dead beyond the fracture. For simple fractures a minimum of support is needed, sometimes no more than transparent tape holding the wing in its normal position or keeping the leg from folding. Splints of matchsticks can be very harsh and cause ulcers or death of the tissue.

DISEASES

Infectious disease can only be successfully diagnosed by the person qualified to do so, the veterinarian. But as a sick

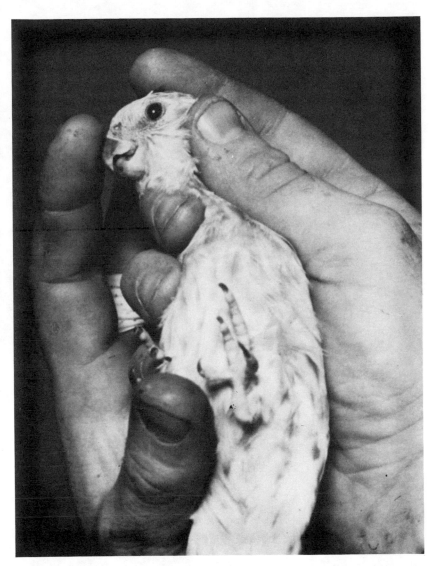

Properly held, a cockatiel can often be induced to open its mouth for inspection if it is nudged gently on the beak. Photo by Miceli Studios.

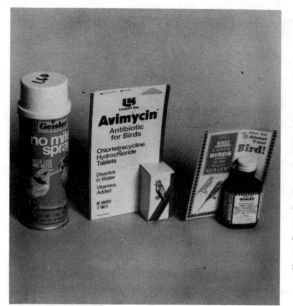

Manufacturers have formulated specific remedies for some of the most common avian ailments, and these remedies—as well as tonics and proprietaries intended to increase birds' resistance to disease in the first place—are obtainable at pet shops dealing in birds and bird supplies.

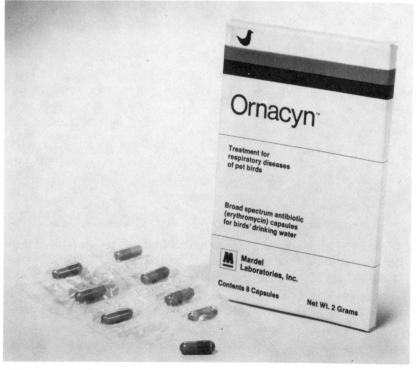

bird with one complaint looks just the same as one suffering from something else, the veterinarian may have more difficulty in determining the complaint than he would with a larger animal. In my experience many cage birds, whether the symptoms be "fits," "loss of feathers," "crusty eyes," or "vague unwellness," are in actuality suffering from a vitamin deficiency. Cage birds in the wild could obtain green food, minerals, animal life and feces. In a cage, few of these things are available. It has often been shown that such ill birds can be restored to health if the diet is broadened and, especially, if some commercial vitamin drops are added to the water.

Very great emphasis is usually given to diarrhea and constipation. Provided that the bird seems in good health, the state of its feces are very likely irrelevant. It is cruel to add laxative medicines to drinking water when constipation, as a disease, probably never affects birds. If diarrhea persists and the bird looks ill, seek expert help. It is unlikely but it could be that the bird is suffering from a complaint that is contagious to humans and delay may increase the risk.

Lastly, people are rightly afraid of contracting psittacosis from a caged parrot. I have never yet encountered a case in a cockatiel. This does not mean that it cannot happen, but I do believe that it is most unlikely, provided that the cockatiel is kept away from other species of parrot.

There is a magnificent book, *Bird Diseases*, by Drs. Arnall and Keymer (TFH). Consult it for any problems you might imagine are afflicting your cockatiel.

Bibliography

Anonymous (Smith, G.A.). *Parrot Society Magazines.* Various articles

Barringer, Clifford. 1960. "Albino Cockatiels," *Foreign Birds: the magazine of the Foreign Bird League,* 26: 146-147.

Bates, H.J. and Busenbark, R.L. 1967. *Parrots and related birds.* 2nd edition. T.F.H. Publications, Neptune, N.J.

Brehm. 1864-1869 *Illustrirte Thierleben.* Volume 3.

Greene, W.T. 1884. *Parrots in Captivity, Vol. 1.* London.

Immelmann, K. 1968. *Australian Parakeets,* A.O.B. Brussels.

Munks, B. 1959. "The dilute Cockatiel," *Foreign Birds: the magazine of the Foreign Bird League* 25:237.

Newton, Alfred. 1893-1896. *A dictionary of birds.* A. & C. Black; London.

Russ, K. 1890?. *The Speaking parrots.* Upcott Gill; London.

Seth-Smith, David. 1902. *Parrakeets.* H. Porter; London.

Smith, G.A. 1976. "Notes on some species of parrot in captivity, *Avicultural Magazine,* 82: 22-28.

West, D.G. 1968. "Pied Cockatiels," *Parrot Society Magazine,* 2: 16-17.

Zann, R. ov. 1965. *Behavioural studies of the Quarrion (nymphicus hollandicus).* Thesis submitted as part of the requirements for the degree of Batchelor of Science with Honours, in the University of New England, Armidale, N.S.W. Australia.

INDEX

Page numbers set in bold type refer to illustrations.